Battle

Battledress

The Uniforms of the World's Great Armies
1700 to the present

Edited by
I. T. SCHICK

Introduction by Alun Chalfont
Illustrated by Wilhelm von Halem

PEERAGE BOOKS

First published in Great Britain by Weidenfeld and Nicolson

This edition published in 1983 by Peerage Books
59 Grosvenor Street
London W1

© 1978 Weidenfeld and Nicolson

ISBN 0 907408 72 9

Printed in Singapore

ENDPAPERS: Prince Eugène
de Beauharnais, highly
respected by his troops,
showed great bravery at the
Battle of Borodino in 1812.

PREVIOUS PAGES: 'The
Battle of Chiari, 1703' by
Dismar Daegen

Contents

Introduction
ALUN CHALFONT

No-one can engage in any prolonged or serious study of military history without becoming familiar with one of its most colourful aspects – the uniform of the soldier through the ages. As military technology has developed and as tactics have changed, uniforms have been transformed from many-splendoured elegance to a functional and almost drab protective camouflage.

In the past the military uniform has fulfilled many purposes. It has served to distinguish the soldier from the civilian, and in this role it has done much, coincidentally, to create and maintain the glamorous reputation traditionally associated with men at arms. This effect was heightened when uniform was used not only to identify soldiers generally, but more specifically to identify the soldiers of one regiment from those of another. When infantry regiments were privately raised by landed gentlemen at their own expense, they were accustomed to design their own uniforms, often as exotic and arresting as the display of plumage of a tropical bird. There was often, too, another affinity with the animal world. When a cat is threatened by an enemy its fur rises to make it look bigger and therefore more formidable. So army uniforms were often designed to give their wearers added stature – tall bearskin hats, broad, square shoulders and heavy leather boots.

All this combined, at one time, to give soldiers a special place in society and a special image in the minds of the rest of the community. It was this image which led Dr Samuel Johnson to remark that every man thinks less of himself for not having been a soldier; and, at a more frivolous level, led one of Charles Dickens's characters to say to another: 'We know, Mr. Weller, we, who are men of the world, that a good uniform must work its way with the women, sooner or later.'

More recently, uniform has reflected a more practical and disenchanted view of the profession of arms. On the modern battlefield it is less important to be able to distinguish the men of a particular regiment than to ensure that soldiers can melt into the surrounding countryside – whether it is jungle, desert or just mud. Lightness and mobility have become the essential characteristics of battledress. As a result uniforms have become austere, colourless and functional. Inevitably they are less frequently used outside combat or training, and off duty the modern soldier melts into the civilian community as effortlessly as he conceals himself on the battlefield. It is perhaps partly as a result of this that the soldier in society has lost some of his glamour and prestige.

All this, however, is in the realm of speculation. The book which follows engages on a more detailed and factual study of the military uniform and its development over the past two centuries. It follows the evolution of uniform from the beginning of the eighteenth century to the armies of the nuclear age, discussing both the history and the psychology of military dress. It is a valuable work of reference for the student of military affairs, and the text is brought alive through some remarkably detailed and beautifully coloured original drawings by Wilhelm von Halem, a German painter who has made a life-long study of uniforms.

The book begins with a prologue by Ruth Bleckwenn, in which she sets the scene with a brief essay on the origins of uniform and its development up to the middle of the seventeenth century when the characteristics of contemporary military dress first began to emerge. Hans Bleckwenn then takes the story through the Wars of European Succession in the first half of the eighteenth century, with its dazzlingly uniformed Hungarian hussars, and the

Guards of Potsdam who kept as a shameful secret the dyeing of their white gaiters to a darker colour before marching out to battle. A team of expert contributors now guide the reader through the French Revolution, the American War of Independence, the American Civil War and the great European wars of the nineteenth century, and there is a useful 'half-way' summing up by John Mollo, who describes the evolution of the mass armies between 1815 and 1860.

Finally Guido Rosignoli, a specialist in modern military history, deals with the twentieth century in three chapters on the First and Second World Wars and the Armies of the Atomic Age, which bring the reader all the way from the tall cap of the eighteenth-century grenadier, designed to enable him to sling his rifle over his shoulder and leave both hands free to prime his grenade, to ALICE (the All-Purpose Lightweight Individual Carrying Equipment of the American soldier in Vietnam).

It is a long journey, and a fascinating one. For those already interested in the subject of military uniform (and they are many) this is a book to delight and illuminate. For the student of military history it has much of great value to offer, especially in its meticulously researched illustrations. Finally, it contains some interesting insights into the more general aspects of military affairs, of which possibly the most thought-provoking occurs in the last paragraph of the last chapter.

We are now far from the days when uniforms were used as a means of distinguishing friend from foe on the battlefield and the modern soldier is often engaged in controlling civil unrest, an unfair role for a uniformed man. Perhaps, eventually, the wearing of uniform may be restricted to ceremonial occasions, and we will be back to the beginning, when the soldier possessed only one uniform.

Or, as Malvolio might have said (and he knew a colourful uniform when he saw one) the whirligig of time brings in its revenges.

Prologue
RUTH BLECKWENN

A soldier's uniform today must be comfortable. It must also (for an infantryman at least) camouflage the wearer, and it must show usually his service and rank. As well as this, we have come to regard absolute uniformity within a single group of men as so essential a characteristic of military dress that 'uniform' has become the everyday term for it.

Military dress was not always governed by these distinguishing factors. Comfort – by the standards of the time – was indeed sometimes considered in earlier centuries. Thus the sixteenth-century trooper dispensed with the civilian's distinctive heavy overcoat and replaced the fashionable padded knee-breeches with loose, baggy trousers: just two examples among many. Despite such specific cases, the design of military uniforms in the past seems to the modern eye to have paid little attention to comfort, and it was not until the twentieth century that this became a major consideration – as was the case with European clothing generally.

Uniform acquired a protective colouring too, only in the twentieth century, shortly before the First World War, simultaneously with the introduction of smokeless powder and long-range, rapid-firing weaponry. Until that time the 'glamour of uniform' had been the distinctive mark of the soldier's trade. Even so, the uniforms of earlier centuries had offered a measure of protection against cut and thrust. Originally the armour of the medieval knight had fulfilled this function. But an infantryman could not wear the heavy chain mail, and from the end of the fifteenth century it was necessarily replaced by the cuirass, which at least protected the torso, or by waistcoats, either lined with or made from some strong material such as leather or thick felt. But this protection availed little against bullets,

and so fell into disuse towards the end of the seventeenth century, when the outcome of events on the battlefield was decided by the use of firearms.

At about the same time, though for different reasons, military dress evolved into 'uniform' – that is, it became standardized within each individual country, unit or rank as to design, colouring and trimmings. This phenomenon was the product of the standing armies of absolutism, and had – as will be seen later – economic as well as social causes.

One function however has been fulfilled by military uniform all down the centuries, and still is today: it distinguishes the fighting man from the civilian (apart from partisans), and identifies his rank and branch of the service, as well as, usually, his nationality and unit.

Thus the knight of the High Middle Ages wore over his generally indistinctive chain mail a knee- or calf-length surcoat, in the colours of his house and usually emblazoned with his armorial bearings as well. His helmet, his shield and the trappings of his horse usually bore the same device, which in the days of hand to hand combat sufficed to make him recognized by all the armies of Europe. Towards the end of the Middle Ages, as armies grew larger, the knight abandoned his own colours for those of his feudal lord or 'party'. Gradually, the waist of the surcoat was narrowed, in keeping with contemporary fashion, and with the design of the new heavy armour the wide pleated flaps were deliberately calculated to emphasize the contrasting slenderness of the waist.

Towards the end of the fifteenth century, warfare, and with it the soldier's dress, underwent a complete change. Armour was no longer adequate protection against the increasing power of archery, and the complex code of chivalry was scattered to the winds by the introduction of the infantry. But the professional armies raised in this period were not only distinguished by a new way of fighting (on foot, attacking and defending in massed ranks); in addition the mercenaries who made up the armies came to form a new social class with its own distinctive characteristics. The mercenaries may have seen themselves as the heirs of the knights (and in terms of self-satisfaction they certainly had nothing to learn from their predecessors), but they were professional soldiers, owing no feudal allegiance, whose contracts became invalid when payment ceased. The soldier of this period was not fighting for an ideal (like the knight before him), or for a nation (like the volunteer of the nineteenth century), but for his own pocket – for wages and plunder. Free of the restrictions of urban society, he lived as an outsider on the fringe of a world which, despite its many tensions, was socially a relatively close-knit one. The only rules by which his life was ordered were those imposed from within his own group.

His dress reflected this unique status. While civilian and peasant had their sartorial wings clipped by sumptuary laws, the soldier's dress blossomed into the realms of the fantastic. True, the design of individual garments was taken from contemporary fashion: he wore a close-fitting doublet, cut low at the neck, with heavy, full sleeves (and usually with a strikingly short flap); under this he wore a full, white, long-sleeved shirt and fairly tight knee-breeches; tight stockings, wide heel-less shoes and a cap completed his costume, as they did a civilian's. But it was the details that characterized the soldier.

As early as the fifteenth century the Swiss infantry had been in the habit of making their long, tight breeches by sewing together strips of different coloured materials – imitating and surpassing the

mi-parti of court dress. But after the turn of the century imagination was given greater scope by the idea of slashing the material, allowing the different colours underneath to show through. This idea too was borrowed by the soldier from civilian fashion, but was exaggerated to the extent that it became the hallmark of military style. The slashing often varied in length, breadth,

A medieval knight from the Manesse Manuscript by Hartmann von Aue, early fourteenth century. The armorial bearings of this knight on his charger are particularly striking.

This battle scene from *Der Weisskunig*, 1516–18 (probably by Hans Burgkmeier the Elder), illustrates the variety of battledress worn by the soldier of this period.

direction and shape within a single garment, often being deliberately asymmetric. Doublet, hose, vest, even shoes and cap could be decorated in this way. As if this were not enough, the practice of using adjacent strips of different-coloured material was not forgotten – and at least some of the material might itself be patterned. Nor did the soldier conceal all this colourful finery beneath the civilian's ample, unslashed coat. Thus every outfit worn by every soldier had its individual character. Moreover this clothing was his own property, bearing no indications of the country for which he fought. Such markings would be superfluous in the new style of battle, with great masses of men opposed to one another.

His pleasure in his slashed clothing did not however make the soldier entirely oblivious of the danger he faced from enemy weapons; over or under his doublet he wore an iron cuirass, or at least a short padded or leather jerkin. Emblems of rank, too, did not quite disappear. Officers fought for the most part on horseback, retaining their armour and often the surcoat too, though more as a symbol of their status than for protection, or as an emblem of their family or liege lord. Senior infantrymen (the forerunners of the later NCOs) also stood out, with their conspicuously plain, unslashed long surcoats, like the knights', but with sleeves.

The knightly dress of surcoat and mail was perpetuated not only by the officers but also by the cavalry (whose tactical role was now of rather reduced importance) – small wonder, since they were almost exclusively recruited from the ranks of the nobility.

From the middle of the sixteenth century the soldier's dress began to change. The doublet became tighter in the sleeves and closer-fitting at the waist, in accordance with contemporary fashion. The breeches, on the other hand, evolved in a very distinctive manner. The very long, loose inner part made of light material was confined by tight knee-length bands, between which the inner material emerged to hang down to the calves. These *Pluderhose*, an invention of the common soldier, were in Germany adopted by civilians, and even by the nobility. The cavalryman, however, rejected this extravagance in favour of more practical, tighter, shorter breeches and long boots; he also began, gradually, to shed his armour. But in general the soldier remained loyal to his brilliant, slashed, parti-coloured plumage.

Towards the end of the sixteenth century the soldier's social standing underwent another change; so too did military tactics. A new military code replaced the soldier's former independence with a system of clear discipline, and formalized tactics led to the introduction of drill, probably necessary anyway with the growing importance of the musket, a complex weapon to handle. The

Jakob de Gheyn's musketeer from *Wapenhandlinghe* . . . 1607. The musketeer usually wore a leather jerkin and a broad-rimmed hat.

ravages of the Thirty Years' War slowed down this development, but could not altogether halt it.

No wonder, then, that around 1600 the dress of the simple infantryman appears relatively plain – gone are the slashed, patterned materials and the glimpses of coloured lining showing through. But again the garments correspond to those in contemporary civilian fashion, the short close-fitting doublet and the loose breeches gathered at the knee. Smooth stockings and low-heeled shoes complete the picture.

It was at this time, too, that the different branches of the service began to adopt distinctive uniforms. The pikeman wore a cuirass and helmet as defence against the cavalry sabre, while the musketeer favoured a leather jerkin and a broad-rimmed hat. The cavalry became modernized: the old full armour had finally dwindled to a cuirass, worn over the clothing, and the cavalryman also showed a preference – probably on practical grounds – for tighter breeches and long boots.

In the first half of the seventeenth century, especially during the Thirty Years' War, changing fashion brought about further alterations in military dress. Between 1620 and 1630 the collar, sleeves and body of the doublet or waistcoat all became wider, while breeches tended to become narrower and tighter. At the same time even the common soldier began to show a renewed taste for finery, now however consisting of ribbons, rosettes, lace trimmings and buttons. But he eschewed the cloak or cassock which the fashionable cavalier tossed casually across his shoulders; this was replaced, of necessity, by the more practical knee-length coat, buttoned in front.

The clothing of officers at this period is worth particular attention, as it became distinct from cavalry dress as a logical consequence of social progress. With the bourgeoisie beginning to penetrate the ranks of the cavalry, the higher ranks in all European armies became more and more the exclusive preserve of the nobility. The officer distinguished himself from his men by a more lavish way of dress, decorated with extra lace, ribbons and rosettes. Also (as with the fashionable civilian), his shirt came back more into the picture, as the fuller sleeves of the doublet opened up, or consisted only of a single strip of material. But the officer's most important badge of rank on the battlefield was his sash (in the colours of his commander) and – a relic of chivalry – the former neck armour, the so-called gorget. His clothing announced, too, that the military élite did not fight on foot, for he proudly wore the badges of horsemanship – tight knee- or calf-length trousers and spurred leather boots. On the field of battle he normally replaced the cuirass with a jerkin of elk leather; on more peaceful occasions he replaced jerkin and waistcoat with a sleeved jacket, buttoned in front, which towards the end of the war became shorter and lost its flared lower part. This manner of dress, a mixture of a baroque love of delicate detail with a common-sense reaction to the harsh realities of warfare, became the model for male fashion in Europe between about 1630 and 1650.

If the officer still had relatively broad scope in the exact way he chose to dress, the clothing of the simple infantryman became, towards mid-century, increasingly plain and uniform. On the one hand, decorative trimmings were reduced; on the other, coloured material became less bright and less varied, with the beiges and browns of natural leather becoming particularly popular. With the benefit of hindsight, we can see here, already, the beginnings of modern military uniform.

European Wars of Eighteenth Century Absolutism 1700-63

1

HANS BLECKWENN

The economic pressures of the Thirty Years' War showed the value of uniform mass production of clothing and weapons. For the 'uniform' to be established as a lasting concept, an important event had first to take place: the rise to supremacy of the absolute monarch over the largely noble 'estates' of his people. The symbol of this new supremacy in every country was the *miles perpetuus*, the standing army. This was both the instrument and the expression of monarchical power, and so had to be both strong and representative. As a lasting institution it had to be financed by money raised from the population in taxes, or – in the case of economically weak nations – raised on loan from wealthy major powers. This was the sociological background of the standing army for over a century; then changing ideas, followed by the brutal demands of a changing technology, set new standards for the relationship between government and defence.

The armies of the eighteenth century were composed of professional soldiers; they were the only insurance for the absolute power of their masters. Volunteers were never available in sufficient numbers, apart from in a few poor, relatively densely populated areas such as Oberhessen and Switzerland. So the armies were brought up to strength with pressed men recruited by more or less violent means, each state having its own special system for the purpose; the choicest abuse was reserved for Prussia, whose 'Soldier King' Frederick William I (1713–40) had tall, powerfully-built men hunted down by force all over Europe. He realized that a long muzzle-loading gun shot farther and straighter than a short one, but that it could only be loaded fast enough by well-drilled soldiers with exceptional reach. While building up his highly effective army he also organized a planned

'The Battle of Höchstädt, 1704', painted and engraved by Jean Huchtenburg at The Hague, gives a view of that part of the battlefield where the day was decided, the left bank of the Danube between Blenheim and Höchstädt.

state economy, abolished serfdom for his peasants and laid the foundations of compulsory national service: the 'native' half of his army spent seven-eighths of the year working at home as civilians, while the other half – a few volunteers and a great many foreign pressed men – was kept as a standing cadre to train each year's fresh recruits; only during the 'exercise period' of from six to eight weeks did the entire army assemble, remaining together until the closing 'royal parade'.

In England the army was small – not for nothing had Parliament executed a king and curbed the absolutist powers of his successors – but the press-gangs of the Royal Navy were the worst imaginable. In Russia the practice was to raise roughly twice as many recruits as the forces required, since half of them were generally lost when marching to the mustering areas. And in Austria sanitary conditions in the southern garrisons were sometimes so bad that the army lost as many men in peacetime as it did in war; training regulations there were frequently concerned with making use of the uniforms of the dead, very rarely with the provision of new ones. Better conditions prevailed in Hanover, whose small army was well administered on the English model, and in Hessen-Kassel, where the straitened economic circumstances meant that younger sons were eager to serve in those units which were so sought after as mercenary forces by the great powers because of their efficiency. In all countries conditions were better socially for the cavalry than for the infantry (we shall see later why this was); specialist troops had no significant part to play until the Seven Years' War (1756–63).

The Thirty Years' War left a legacy of military solidarity in Europe's armies that transcended political ideas and frontiers: it was quite customary for an officer to change allegiances, for his men to desert from one army to another. But this 'soldiers' union' also handed down a code of ideas, rules and traditions, including some relics of chivalric ideals, which contributed to the humanization of warfare in the eighteenth century – from the special concept of honour (the duel) to rules of behaviour towards civilians, the wounded and prisoners – rules which were eventually enshrined in the Geneva and Hague Conventions.

Most importantly, the different armies of the early eighteenth century remained similar in their way of life and appearance, so that comparisons can be drawn and a general view obtained.

Ever since the crossbow (and not gunpowder) had brought about the decline in the use of armour, the infantry became the decisive factor on the battlefield. Able to make use of the rapid technical advances in weaponry, it gradually became more important than the cavalry, restricted as the latter was to the limited natural abilities of the horse. From 1700 onwards, then, the infantry may be regarded as the main arm of the service, and so it will be examined first.

Style in military uniform is strongly influenced by military success, as surely as in civilian life it follows fashion. Because France emerged from the Thirty Years' War as the undoubted victor, from 1670 the European soldiers adopted the *justaucorps*, or long woollen coat. Originally French peasant costume, it had been adopted by the French army, and then found its way into civilian fashion. Although after 1718 the uniform coat began, under Prussian influence, to differ in cut from the civilian, it remained the basis of military dress, and was the more enthusiastically taken back into civilian use as armies came to be composed not only of professionals but of civilian levies as well.

To be suitable as a uniform, this coat

PRUSSIA

Musketeer NCO of the 1st
Guards Battalion (15th
Regiment), 1806

Grenadier of the Grena-
dier Guards Battalion
(6th Regiment), 1806

Grenadier, 1st Guards
Battalion

Grenadier of the 7th
Infantry Regiment (von
Bevern's), 1757

Officer of the 5th Infantry
Regiment (Duke Ferdinand
of Brunswick's), 1757

PRUSSIA

Musketeer of von
Knobloch's Infantry
Regiment

Fusilier of Prince Regent
Henry of Prussia's Fusilier
Regiment

Musketeer of Forçade de
Biaix's Infantry Regiment
(23rd)

Fusilier of the 48th
Fusilier Regiment (Crown
Prince of Hessen-Kassel's)

Musketeer of the 18th
Infantry Regiment (Prince
of Prussia's)

PRUSSIA

Hussar of the 2nd Hussar Regiment (von Zieten's),

Bosniak, 1760

Hussar of the 7th Hussar Regiment (von Malachowski's) wearing the pelisse, 1762

Hussar of the 1st Hussar Regiment (von Kleist's), 1762

Officer of the 7th Hussar Regiment (von Malachowski's)

PRUSSIA

Dragoon of the 11th (Jung von Platen's) Dragoon Regiment, 1762

Cuirassier of the 2nd Cuirassier Regiment (Prince of Prussia's), 1757

Officer of the 8th Cuirassier Regiment (von Seydlitz's), 1762

Officer of the 11th Dragoon Regiment (Jung von Platen's), 1762

Mounted Cuirassier of the Leibregiment (3rd), 1762

PRUSSIA

Staff Officer of the 2nd Hussar Regiment (von Zieten's), 1762

Hussar of Kleist's Freihusar, 1760

Officer of the Gardes du corps Regiment in gala uniform

Dragoon of Gachray's Freikorps, 1761

Adjutant of the Cavalry

PRUSSIA

Chasseur of the Corps of Foot Chasseurs

Gunner of the Foot Artillery, 1757

Officer of the 39th Fusilier Regiment (Prince Frederick Francis of Brunswick's), 1757

Officer of the 3rd Garrison Battalion (von Grolmann's), 1757

Chasseur of Favrat's Freikorps, 1762

GREAT BRITAIN

Musketeer, 2nd Regiment of Foot (The Buffs), 1742

Musketeer, 28th Infantry Regiment (28th Foot), 1742

Grenadier of the 1st Regiment of Guards, 1745

Grenadier of the 20th Regiment of Foot, 1759

Grenadier of the 21st Regiment Royal Scots Fusiliers, 1742

GREAT BRITAIN

11th Dragoon Regiment, Dragoon of the Light Squadron, 1757

2nd Dragoon Guards, 1760

Dragoon of the 17th Light Dragoon Regiment, 1761

6th Regiment of Horse, 1742

Royal Horse Guards (The Blues), 1742

GREAT BRITAIN

Gunner of the Royal
Artillery, 1742–56

42nd Regiment of Foot
(Highlanders), 1745

Grenadier of the 1st
Squadron of Mounted
Grenadier Guards, 1750

Officer of the 1st Guards
Regiment, 1745

Light Infantry in North
America, 1758

HANOVER

Grenadier of von Freytag's
Freikorps, 1760

Grenadier of the Guards
Regiment, 1759

Musketeer Officer of
Hardenberg's Regiment,
1759

Grenadier of von
Scheither's Infantry
Regiment, 1756

Foot Chasseur of von
Freytag's Freikorps, 1760

HANOVER

Grenadier Officer of von Müller's Dragoon Regiment, 1761

Mounted Chasseur of von Freytag's Freikorps, 1760

Mounted Grenadier, 1743

Carabinier of von Scheither's Freikorps, 1762

Hussar of Luckner's Freikorps, 1762

GERMAN STATES

Palatinate, officer of Count von Hatzfeld's Carabinier Regiment, 1740

Bavaria, Grenadier of the Leib Regiment, 1740

Schaumburg-Lippe, Carabinier of the Carabinier Corps, 1756

Hessen-Kassel, Grenadier of Count von Hessenstein's Infantry Regiment, 1749

Saxe-Gotha, Garde du corps, 1756

GERMAN STATES

Franconian District, Ferentheil Infantry Regiment, Grenadier, 1760

Electorate of Cologne, Grenadier, 1757

Wurttemberg, District Regiment of Foot, 1756

Upper Rhine District, Grenadier of the Hessen-Darmstadt Regiment, 1753

Swabian District, Grenadier of the Baden-Baden Infantry Regiment, 1760

GERMAN STATES

Bavaria, Dragoon of the Piosasque Regiment of Dragoons, 1748

Wurttemberg, Foot Grenadier, 1750

Hessen-Darmstadt, Dragoon of the Guards Dragoon Regiment, 1750

Hessen-Darmstadt, Trooper of the Mounted Leibgarde, 1750

Franconian District, Deutschordens Dragoon Regiment, 1757

LEFT 'The Battle of
Fontenoy, 1745' by Van
Blarenberghe. An officer
makes his report to the king
(*right*) while a column of
British and Hanoverian
infantry is attacked by the
French cavalry and guns.

OVERPAGE 'Une halte de la
Maison du Roi' by Charles
von Parrocel (1688–1752).
The king's grenadiers stop
for a rest.

SAXONY

Musketeer of von
Rochow's Regiment of
Infantry, 1754

Grenadier of the Leib
Grenadier Guards, 1750

Major-General of Cavalry

Cuirassier of O'Byrn's
Cuirassier Regiment, 1748

Artilleryman, 1740

SWEDEN

Infantry drummer, 1765

NCO of the Södermannland
Infantry Regiment, 1765

Trooper of the Norra
Skanska Cavalry
Regiment, 1757

Södermannland Infantry
Regiment, 1756

Hussar of the Yellow
Regiment, 1762

AUSTRIA

Officer of Joseph
Esterhazy's (Hungarian)
Infantry Regiment, 1742

Grenadier of the
Saxe-Gotha (Dutch)
Infantry Regiment, 1762

Infantryman of Lascy's
(German) Infantry
Regiment, 1762

Infantryman of
Simbschen's (Hungarian)
Infantry Regiment, 1762

Grenadier of Haller's
(Hungarian) Infantry
Regiment, 1762

AUSTRIA

Officer of the
Peterwardein National
Frontier Infantry
Regiment, 1750–7

German Artillery Corps,
1765

Engineer Officer, 1765

Officer of the Slavonic
Gradisca National Frontier
Infantry Regiment, 1765

Chasseur of the
Sharpshooters Corps, 1762

AUSTRIA
Dragoon of Batthiani's
Dragoon Regiment, 1762

Cuirassier of de Ville's
Cuirassier Regiment,

Dragoon of the Hessen-
Darmstadt Dragoon
Regiment, 1762

Cuirassier of the
Trauttmansdorf Cuirassier
Regiment, 1762

Dragoon of St Ignon's
Dragoon Regiment,
1762–3

AUSTRIA
Trumpeter of von
Kalnoky's Hussar
Regiment, 1762

Pandour of Trenck's
Corps, 1762

Hussar of the 'Emperor'
Hussar Regiment, 1762

Hussar of Esterhazy's
Hussar Regiment in
pelisse, 1762

Hussar of Baranyay's
Hussar Regiment

FRANCE

Grenadier of the Royal-
Lorraine Infantry Regiment

Infantryman of the Dillon
Regiment, c. 1761

Guardsman of the Hundred
Swiss (c. 1740–5)

Infantry officer, 1747

Infantryman of the Nassau-
Saarbrücken Infantry
Regiment, 1750

FRANCE

1st (French) Company of
the Gardes du corps, 1757

Schomberg's Dragoons,
1757

Grenadier of the Royal
Allemand Mounted
Grenadier Regiment,
1750

Uhlan of Marshal de
Saxe's Volunteers, 1745

Hussar of the
Nassau-Saarbrücken
Hussar Regiment, 1757

RUSSIA
Musketeer in full dress uniform, 1763–6

Grenadier of the St Petersburg Division in sleeved tunic, 1762

Infantry Officer, 1762

Grenadier, 1762

Gunner of the Artillery, 1757

RUSSIA
Hussar of the Hungarian Hussar Regiment, 1741–64

Grenadier Officer of the Dragoon Guards, 1756

Cuirassier, 1756–62

Dragoon, 1756–62

Hussar of the Moldavian Hussar Regiment, 1741–64

needed certain distinctive colourings. Its base colour distinguished one army from another; and different-coloured linings could be used to distinguish between regiments, especially if some parts of the coat were folded back to show the inside. In those early days aesthetic and practical considerations went together happily enough; mass-produced textiles were still rather loosely woven and it was quite natural to protect the particularly vulnerable edges by turning them back.

Thus the sleeve acquired a cuff, the neck a collar and the chest a lapel; the word 'facing' itself was used either for the turned-back part of the coat-tail, or generally for any of these embellishments, for the eighteenth century was not particularly fussy about terminology. The style of facings varied in any case, and it was customary to name each individual type after the army that had first adopted it, or simply favoured it.

Although military dress had long since diverged from the civilian it continued to follow very general tendencies in fashion, not only in changing heights of waistband and breadth of coat-tail or sleeve; even the facings were loosely based on contemporary taste. The picture is complicated by the fact that Prussia, in the course of the reforms of 1718, had deliberately turned aside from developing European taste: marked changes in uniform, immediately adopted by the civilian population of Prussia, reflected new economic and social ideas.

Even more complicated is the relationship between uniform and fashion in colour. Occasionally a particular group adopted a highly individual colour. One example was the Austrian *de Ligne* regiment: its gallant Walloons were known everywhere for the very striking pink they favoured for their insignia. Generally, how-

ever, choice of colour in military matters was limited by practical considerations. The black clouds of smoke over the battlefields required bright colours to enable the disposition of troops to be visible. Only occasionally did an impulse of heraldic tradition break through – as for instance when a troop's coats and facings chanced to harmonize with its banners; but unfortunately we often do not know what exactly was green about a 'Green Regiment' of the seventeenth century. Later only small armies – like the Swedes after 1720, with their generally yellow insignia on blue coats – clung to the heraldic colours.

It is claimed of the blue coats of Brandenburg, on the other hand, that only this colour could effectively conceal the exceptionally poor and uneven quality of local woollen cloth. In that case we would expect the undyed grey (later whitish) *Iglauer* cloth worn by the Imperial troops to be of better

The French Royal Grenadiers, seen here encamped in 1757, wore white uniforms, a colour also adopted by the Italians, Hungarians and Spanish in the eighteenth century.

quality. White was well suited to the climate in the imperial garrisons in Hungary and Italy, and France and Spain also preferred this colour for their infantry. Whether this was deliberate or purely accidental is hard to tell, for it is in the south, curiously, that fur caps also survived. In the north-west, Great Britain, with Hanover and Denmark, favoured red – perhaps because it was the colour of the 'Berserkers', the Norse warriors who would rush into battle clad only in a coat of red paint. In any event, the Scots and the Irish took their red colours with them into the foreign regiments of the Franch army, where it mingled with the blue of northern and central Europe imported by the Germans. The Russian infantry dressed in green; England and Prussia competed for the contract in St Petersburg, and the difficulty of making an even, long-lasting green dye gave the Russian commissariat admirable opportunities to haggle over the merchandise and force the prices down.

Blue was the cheapest colour to use, even when the native woad had been supplanted by imported indigo. Red madder was rather dearer, but England, Hanover and Denmark could afford it for their relatively small armies. Pink and carmine, like green, were difficult to produce in even, lasting quality, and therefore expensive because of the risks involved for the contractor. Mourning black is not to the soldier's taste, unless deliberately adopted to denote defiance of death. So the battlefields of the century were dominated by white and by red, blue and yellow, the latter being a popular colour for nether garments – probably in imitation of the traditional painted buff leather.

Finally, colour also had a social significance. White linings in Prussia up to 1713 distinguished the Guards, while blue denoted the royal regiments in both France and England. Green everywhere stood for chasseurs, who, as the first light troops in the modern sense, were highly regarded in time of war, while red was the badge of nobility – around 1700 in some countries not only generals but whole officer corps wore red coats, even when their men were dressed in other colours. In Prussia this custom persisted until 1914, and even today the red coat survives on the hunting field.

The choice of colour for facings remained the privilege of the regimental commander, the more tenaciously with the survival of the old aristocracy as a force in the state. In Prussia the colours were fixed by 1700, in Austria not until 1763. But as well as commanding officer and sovereign there gradually arose the third force, that of tradition, when a regiment's proud memories became associated with specific eccentricities of their uniform.

This was even truer of the various embellishments on uniform, which included not only buttons in varying numbers and positions, but more especially the trimmings of lace, braid and – for officers – embroidery. Buttons might be yellow (brass) or white (pewter), the COs and NCOs of the unit being distinguished by gold or silver respectively. In the early days numerous buttons were worn with no purpose other than decoration – with the coat having at first a single row on the right, later a row on each side, both styles having survived until today in men's wear, with Europe buttoning left over right and Asia vice versa – as we can see in the case of the hussars. A French speciality was to adorn the pocket-flaps of the coat with a motley assortment of buttons.

Even the metal of which buttons were made had its own regulations: because the pewter was less hard-wearing than brass, even the 'white' regiments had yellow buttons on their gaiters, where the most wear could be expected. In Prussia, white metal was forbidden until 1740, because of the 'Soldier King's' loathing for every aspect of Regency style, which favoured silver. Silver he allocated to the despised non-combatants, like the Quartermaster, and the medical and legal specialists. When Crown Prince Frederick – later Frederick the Great – took the exceptional step of decreeing white metal for his own regiment in 1732, it was seen as a sign of a political inclination towards France – and rightly so, as his alliance with France against Prussia in 1740 was to demonstrate.

In the seventeenth and eighteenth centuries, it was both the duty and the privilege of a servant to wear colourful braid on his coat; so too with the soldier, who paid for his own uniform with deductions from his pay. For the common soldier the braid was generally of wool, elaborately patterned and often in the personal colours of the commanding officer of the regiment. Particularly rich was that worn by the band, who were regarded as the personal employees first of the company commander and later of the regimental commanding officer; the so-called 'swallow's nest' worn by the Germans is a survival of this former splendour. The NCOs were distinguished by metal braid, while officers' coats were often embroidered. At first this embroidery was widely spread over the front of the coat; later it came to be concentrated on the lapels and round the buttonholes, for braid – like the facings – often served the practical purpose of strengthening the more vulnerable parts of a garment. When braid began to disappear from the edges of the coat the loops – originally the edging around the buttonholes – remained behind.

This taste for braid not only diminished as time went on, but also showed from the beginning a marked variation between north and south England, and Hanover and Hessen-Kassel which followed their lead aesthetically as well as politically retained braid edgings and loops until the Seven Years' War, Prussia kept loops until 1806, while the 'white south', Russia and Sweden, made only sparing use of this embellishment.

Wars soon put paid to all this splendour, as we can see in the case of Hanover around 1760. Only in Prussia was it a part of the planned economy (for instance the military orphanage at Potsdam was given the monopoly on the manufacture of gold and silver lace), so in 1763 the old Prussian regiments still looked as they did in 1756, though the 'new' regiments raised after 1740 wore plain uniforms from the start.

For similar economic reasons Prussia was from 1725 onwards the only country in Europe to issue new uniforms to the army every year. If this meant the 'mothballing' of numerous uniforms, the soldier's ownership of his own coat meant that all these relatively new cast-offs were soon determining the style of the national dress. The intermediary between army and economy was the 'General Clothing Office' in Berlin which planned the ordering of uniforms from manufacturers throughout the country according to the individual requirements of each regiment, and with the aid of a central 'braid pattern book' which is still maintained. The manufacturer was paid out of the regiment's annual allocation of clothing funds, and economy was maintained by the careful supervision of finances. So it is not so astonishing that in 1757, despite a highly critical overall situation, the army halted for a whole valuable day in Torgau, on its march from Rossbach in Thuringia to Leuthen in Silesia, to receive the new uniforms which had been brought up the Elbe. In Prussia nothing was paid for until it was delivered.

Other countries issued new uniforms

every two or three years, and frequently a longer interval would be allowed to elapse. They vacillated for decades between the idea of having the representative body order uniforms (especially in Austria) and a system of *ad hoc* contracts between commanding officers and private contractors – a laborious, extravagant and unsatisfactory system.

Having considered the uniform coat, the most important part of military dress, at some length, we now turn to other features.

Since uniforms then had turned-down rather than high collars, the cravat or stock formed part of the uniform and its colour was controlled. It might be red, black or white – red being reserved for the other ranks, while black came into general use in the course of the century. In Prussia, red (white for officers) distinguished the 'old' regiments, while the 'new' ones raised after 1740 wore black, as did the Royal Guard and all cavalry units. In Austria red and black existed side by side, and for large-scale parades the regiments agreed to stick to one or the other for the sake of uniformity.

The 'nether garments' consisted of waist-coat and knee-breeches, the former conforming to the general trend in contemporary tailoring, gradually becoming shorter and tighter. The waistcoat had pockets, and often sleeves, though the latter were sometimes dispensed with in summer. To save wear and tear on the expensive coat, everyday duties in summer were generally carried out in the waistcoat only; the Russian infantry acquired during its campaigns on the steppes the habit of marching and fighting in waistcoats, while coats were left behind with the baggage. Instead they carried a light cloak, which in good weather was worn rolled up as a bandolier or slung round the back of the neck with the ends tucked under the belt over each hip.

Breeches were knee-length; only troops of Hungarian nationality or origin wore them ankle-length, a development of old-fashioned hose. Both types laced up in front and were fastened at the hip, as one sees today in Alpine local costume.

Originally these clothes were usually made of buff leather, which lasted well and would offer some protection against a casual sword-blow or nearly spent bullet; on the other hand, it was also stiff, difficult to manipulate, and not warm enough. Cloth began to replace leather in the infantry early in the eighteenth century. The cloth was often dyed in the regimental colours – especially red – but later in the century white and shades of yellow became ever more predominant; in Austria in 1756, for instance, half the army was still wearing regimental colours, but by 1762 almost all units had switched to white. The habit of *Kollern*, that is, colouring these clothes with various earth colours, was a surviving legacy of the days of leather. An additional issue of linen trousers for warm weather was made in some armies.

Woollen stockings were also worn, and for marching in hot weather greased linen socks (tallow rags). In about 1700 coloured stockings became part of regimental distinguishing marks; the diary of a Munster officer watching the French preparations for the War of the Spanish Succession in their camp at Compiègne in 1698 records the stocking colours of each regiment. After 1714 Prussia introduced white linen spatter-dashes – side-buttoned gaiters reaching over the knee – and this fashion soon spread all over Europe. A tight fit looks better, but is inconvenient to the soldier, and 'gaiter service' has since been the German soldier's term for the dour and apathetic discharge of military duties. It was Prussia, too, that introduced the black marching gaiters in the war of 1744 which became general wear in the winter and on service. Only the Guards in Potsdam retained white, and when in 1756 they dyed their gaiters black before marching out, it was kept a strict secret.

Shoes were very like the shoes of today, laced or buckled; only the Hungarian ankle-length trousers required the wearing of ankle-boots. Even here there were farcical touches: in Prussia the toes of shoes had to be cut straight, as only cads and the provost marshal's branch wore round toes – and the Dutch, usually so ardently admired by the 'Soldier King'. In France an officer announced his exalted rank by wearing red heels, and fashionable society delightedly followed suit.

Old pictures can still be dated today from the exact shape of the tricorn hat, which fashion altered constantly from decade to decade. At first the brim was simply opened out while the crown was usually rounded; only in the Netherlands did it retain an obvious felt-hat shape for a while. Around 1730–40 the crown was flattened and the front pulled sharply forward; finally in Austria, for instance, it became the high-brimmed Austrian *Khevenhüller*, while in Prussia it was of more average size, larger in the cavalry than in the infantry. In the second half of the century the peak levelled off more and more, the height of the brim increased, and around 1800 the high bicorne or 'millwheel' evolved, by which time other forms of headgear, which in the first half of the century were found only among the Balkan regiments or special units, had come to predominate.

The normal decoration of the hat was a plain white edging – sometimes scalloped in Austria – and little tassels on the end of the drawstring that held the crown in shape. In addition some armies affected a woollen pom-pom on the left side of the front brim; all three were originally in company colours, later regimental ones, and often of

A soldier of the Austrian Ogulin Regiment in 1757. The Austrians wore a sprig of green oak leaves or fir twigs in their hats to distinguish themselves from the French.

heraldic significance. Instead of a pom-pom, ribbon cockades in national colours were sometimes tied or buttoned to the left side of the front brim, white for the French and Saxons, black for the Prussians and English, and red for the Spaniards. Austrians fighting against France – white against white – wore a spray of green oak leaves in their hats as a distinguishing mark, in winter using fir twigs or even folded green cardboard. As the cardboard was green on one side only, we find Austrian officers as late as 1763 wearing green and white cockades, the spray of leaves being retained only by the hussars.

Another distinguishing mark was the upright tuft of feathers, which later became so popular in all armies, especially among the cavalry. These were first introduced by the Prussians in Silesia in 1762, to remind their new allies the Cossacks to impale their old friends rather than their new ones.

As well as the hat, there was another form of specialized headgear – the forage cap, or bonnet, a development of the pointed civilian nightcap. It achieved fame in its highly stylized form as the grenadier's cap. The hand-grenade, introduced in the seventeenth century, was a hollow shell of splintering material – usually metal, sometimes glass or hard-baked clay – which was filled with powder and detonated by means of a fuse. To light the fuse before throwing the grenade, a man needed both hands free, so that he had to sling his rifle over his shoulder, and a tricorn hat would have been inconvenient. And so the grenadier wore his tall cap, which had only its shape in common with the nightcap. The throwing of the grenade was and remained a tricky business, as the fuses could not be synchronized properly, and grenadier units were always recruited from long-serving, hardened soldiers; the grenadier's cap thus became the symbol of courage and experience. It was soon modified. Depending on whether the cloth band around the cap was trimmed with fur or embellished with a brass emblem, the cap gradually developed through various transitional forms into either a fur cap or a conical metal hat; these varied from army to army, so that at the 'night and fog' battle of Hochkirch in 1758, Austrian and Prussian grenadiers had to tell friend from foe by feeling each other's caps. This two-fold development was unique in that for about fifty years it reflected religious belief: the Catholic countries, despite their warm southerly situation, favoured fur, the Protestants cloth and metal. Yet again, clothing took on a political significance; when the Imperial army was called out against the despised Frederick II of Prussia in 1757, the Franconian Protestants of the Hohenzollern princedoms of Anspach and Bayreuth appeared amongst the Imperial troops in their own 'Prussian' caps instead of the prescribed Franconian bearskins; at Rossbach they fired into the air once and promptly disappeared. Six weeks later, at Leuthen, the extremely Protestant army of Württemberg, who were meant to stop the first Prussian attack, behaved in a similar fashion. Only later did the fur cap really establish itself in military fashion, and is to be seen today outside palaces and castles in London and Copenhagen, the Danes having a small scrap of red cloth at the back as the last reminder of the old 'nightcap'.

A distinctive variation is the fusilier cap, introduced by Prussia in about 1725 and copied by other armies for a long period. Like the grenadier's cap it had a metal peak, but with no pom-pom; instead it had a low hard crown surmounted by a spike. When there were no longer enough tall men to make up further regiments, Prussia had to make do with smaller ones; their firearms were necessarily shorter, and their fighting strength correspondingly less. Grenadier-type caps were intended to conceal these fatal weaknesses, as indeed was the name 'fusilier', which in England, for example, described the élite troops who in about 1690 had been the first to be issued with the new flintlocks instead of the old matchlock muskets.

In the eighteenth century hairstyle was an important part of military dress. The full-bottomed wig, already in decline from 1700, was replaced in Prussia from 1718 onwards by the smaller *Muffer* with its pigtail; the King was occasionally known to throw his generals' wigs on the fire with his own hand. For ceremonial occasions the hair was powdered, and from 1730 the predominant style included elaborately dressed side-curls stiffened with mutton fat. One can distinguish individual regiments according to the number and position of these curls, and once again, Europe adopted the style so that not even the 'French bag' could hold out against the 'Prussian tail'. Moustaches were only found in the ranks, and varied in colour and cut from regiment to regiment, blonde moustaches being the special privilege of a Prussian regiment, while grenadiers and NCOs naturally had to wear extremely fierce and military styles. Among officers moustaches were restricted to the hussars – and had to be suitably fierce. Only very occasionally in a *galerie* of officers does a little black fleck appear on the upper lip of a nonconformist; the 'old Dessauer', the father of Prussian drill, was one exception, and was consequently known as 'old Moustache', or depicted as a tom-cat. The importance attached to hairstyle in the first half of the eighteenth century is clearly shown by reports that on marching into a city whole regiments immediately flocked to have their hair done, or that work went on through the night to produce particularly beautiful styles for a royal inspection. But alas, in 1756 the blast of war shattered the whole spell, and it vanished, never again to return in full glory.

The cavalryman looked down on the mere foot-soldier, for his trade demanded more than just a well-drilled familiarity with a single weapon. A different spirit prevailed among the mounted troops. The heavy *Reuter* was not in fact the last of the knights, for the *Lanzierer* survived until soon after 1600; but he could tell himself it was because he wore a breastplate and, in Austria, the arrows of the Turks kept him wearing a real helmet until as late as 1790. The *Reuter* in fact existed until 1918, but changed his name to *Kürassier*.

The dragoon looked on enviously. His roots were in the infantry, and he was simply given a cheap nag to get him from place to place quickly when he was needed.

He kept his infantryman's coat and his longer-than-average carbine with bayonet, but had no trace of armour. Only at the end of the century did he manage to get rid of the drummer who drummed everywhere on horseback and replace him with a trumpeter; and eventually the 'élite' dragoons were allowed to relinquish their grenadier caps.

Nevertheless the dragoons shared in the popularity of the cavalry; the mounted troops of every army included volunteers; even, in prosperous Hanover, farmers' sons with their own horses. So the cavalry style was something rather different.

The cuirassier too had his coat; but his main item of clothing was the buff leather jacket, which later evolved into a cloth one. Once again the general picture can best be seen by reference to the clearly-organized Prussian army. The thick leather, not easily chafed through by the iron breastplate, came from the East Prussian elk. After the plague of 1708–10 the elk spread deep into the depopulated areas of East Prussia, to be driven back again around 1720 by the planned repopulation programme introduced by the 'Soldier King', when refugees of all descriptions came to start a new life in East Prussia. Now leather became scarce, and a particularly thick, tough woollen cloth known as kersey replaced leather, at least for everyday duties. As the new material proved supple, warm and much more colourful (since it could be embroidered with coloured patterns and emblems) leather was abandoned altogether, though the new jacket, or *Koller* was cut in the same style as the old. For another 150 years the cuirassier fastened it in front with hooks and eyes instead of buttons, and, when it was dirty, redyed it in a natural leather colour, which only gradually gave way to white. The *chemisette* worn underneath was also hooked rather than

A grenadier–drummer of
the Dragoons, around 1740.
He was replaced by a
trumpeter at the end of the
eighteenth century.

buckled, and both garments retained the band of braid on which the hooks and eyes had been fixed on the old leather jerkin.

No one begrudged the cavalry their leather breeches – no one that is except the commissariat, which constantly experimented with cheaper cloth breeches from all over the place, without success. Cuirassiers and dragoons both had heavy boots; only in France did the dragoons remain faithful to their leather gaiters, which buckled at the side. For attacking in closed ranks, horsemen need tough, thick leather padding to protect their knees in the crush; when a cuirassier's head was taken off by a cannonball on the field of Rossbach in 1757, it was not enough to stop him riding back into camp with the rest that evening! Obviously an apocryphal moral tale to encourage the squadron to keep its ranks closed – yet the contemporary source gives the man's name, company and regiment.

Two more peculiarities distinguished the cavalry. First, unlike the infantry, they still wore cloaks, either capes or full-scale overcoats cut in the voluminous style of 1700. When Prussia, and the states that followed Prussia's lead, introduced the cloth jacket, there was no further need for the old long coat; only officers retained it, in the form of a lace-trimmed gala coat, largely for social purposes. All these cavalry coats were for the most part white in the German states, with coloured facings; red in England; red, white or blue in France. The Austrian dragoons also used red, white and blue (and green too in some regiments), while the Prussians changed, from about 1741, from white to the light blue which they retained until 1914. Otherwise cavalry coats were notably plain. The horse made the man; and the horse's trappings stole the show. Saddle-cloths and holster-covers were resplendent in the regimental colours and, particularly in the older mounted regiments,

braid-trimmed edges and ornaments, coats of arms, mottoes or princely monograms were embroidered in the corners in coloured wool; officers went in for lavish embroidery, lacework and fringes of silver and gold, so that a parade saddle-cloth could cost a small fortune.

The geographical perspective of Europe was at first limited to the western and central areas, the old Roman Empire and its successors. So, apart from the Scottish troops, the greatest sensation of the time was caused by those south-eastern races who from 1741 onwards were organized into fighting units of the Austrian armies to take part in the War of the Austrian Succession. The numerous engravers working in Augsburg at the time devoted many a romantic page to them, and the Pandour Trenck is still a familiar figure today. Apart from the celtic national dress of Scotland, which had been known in Germany in the days of Gustavus Adolphus, the sensation was mainly caused by clothing of Asiatic origin.

The Austrian hussars had been familiar figures since 1700 and had been imitated by small corps in other armies, but now the hussars began to appear in massed regiments, dazzlingly uniformed; as well as light and dark blue, green was a familiar basic colour, while from 1740–60 red and even yellow also began to appear. Their impressive uniforms, decked out with white, red or yellow braid, were changed almost as often as the regimental commanders. Prussia developed her hussars from 1741, expanding at a stroke from a mere scattering to eight full regiments, and the colours of their uniforms were laid down once and for all. In matters of detail, however, the commanding officer was allowed a free hand, and the new branch of the service took advantage of this to express its personality. The hussars in Central Europe were light horse (except in Poland, where they were armoured), and were mounted on small, fast, durable horses of Ukrainian stock. Their duties – defence, reconnaissance and skirmishing – required reliable, skilful and intelligent soldiers; and when Prussia, economical as always, decided to train them to be used in massed attacks on the battlefield as well, they took it in their stride.

Hussar and Hungarian were synonymous at first, even in Prussia, whose early hussars were Protestant renegades. Later, when most countries had at least a few hussars in their armies, new recruits came mainly from the homeland, but the élitist spirit of the early days survived. Until 1918 there existed in Germany an especially strong bond of comradeship between hussar and chasseur. In love, too, the hussar was a fast worker; he literally wore his heart on his sleeve (a small heart-shaped leather patch), and the 'faithful hussar' has even been immortalized in song.

Their uniform too remained Hungarian. Apart from a cape for bad weather, the main item of winter clothing was at first the pelisse or short cloak; later an animal skin would be lined with material and then turned inside out. Until 1806 the officers commanding the Prussian Guard Hussar squadrons on parade wore red-lined panther skins with the skin outwards. From 1756, in Prussia, the pelisse was carried at all times, even in battle, where it was worn over the left shoulder as a protection against sword cuts. Like the Hungarian-style jacket or *dolman* the cloak was fastened with buttons and loops. After 1700 these were extended in rows across the breast of both garments, and the braid that formed the loops ran right around the edges of both. The dolman had a small stand-up collar and pointed Hungarian cuffs, which over the years often acquired a different colour from the rest of the garment. The hussar's breeches too were exotic by European standards; they were made of cloth, with distinctive braid trimmings on the front. Boots were calf-length only, since hussars rarely rode in closed ranks; officers' boots were often of yellow leather, while NCOs' were red. The original headgear was a cap, felt in summer, fur in winter; the felt variety usually had a cockade at the front, and a wrap-around 'wing' which the hussar could 'let fly'. The fur cap was low to start with, later becoming higher; from the top hung a bag of coloured cloth, the *kolpak*. The Hungarian saddle-cloth covered the pistol holster at the front, and ended at the back in long points. Finally we must not forget the *sabretache*, which evolved from the ancient quiver: its flat surface was covered with cloth, and allowed room for copious decoration – scalloped edges in a contrasting colour, monograms or coats of arms and in Prussian, of course, the royal monogram. The sabretache was also worn by the Hungarian infantry until the Seven Years' War, and by the Prussian cuirassiers; the hussar's uniform and the cuirassier's jacket had little room for pockets, and what was a cavalryman without his tobacco and pipe?

The Habsburg Hungarian infantry also dressed in their own fashion, with the tricorn hat and coats of the basic German cut. In addition they wore a dolman as a waistcoat and Hungarian pantaloons. Even more faithful to local tradition were the frontiersmen of the Austrian Empire, such as the Serbo-Croat peasant-soldiery along the Turkish border, who probably ranked with the Hessians and Scots as the best soldiers in contemporary Europe. They wore the *klobuk*, a tall cylindrical felt cap which was probably the ancestor of the *Kaskett* worn by Austrian infantry from 1769, and so also of the shako, which was

The Scottish Highlander, a soldier of the 'Black Watch' Regiment, 1745. Engraving by G. Bickham.

later worn everywhere. These borderers 'didn't even have shoes to their feet' – the assertion was true but the inference was not, as their *opanken*, strips of leather wrapped round the feet and secured with string, were more comfortable; if they wanted 'German' shoes, it was only as a status symbol. The Austrian army's official uniforms were too expensive, and they were always reduced to their home-made coats, greyish-white or brown depending on the strain of sheep in the locality; brown later became the basic colour of their uniforms.

The effective but arduous business of fighting with lances was entrusted to the warriors of the south-eastern steppes, the Poles and Cossacks. In about 1745, under sometimes romantic circumstances, there began to spring up small bodies of Uhlans in France (Saxon Volunteers) and Prussia (Bosniaks). The latter wore not only the kaftan, but even the turban. In 1756 the

Seven Years' War threw the Bosniaks into battle against the Cossacks, who were raiding East Prussia. Here they showed what they could do, and their ranks were soon swelled with Mohammedan renegades, when in 1760 the Sublime Porte was considering a holy war on Prussia's behalf. After the partition of Poland the Islamic gentry of the new areas – Westpreussen, between Pommern and Ostpreussen, and Südpreussen, in the south of Ostpreussen – replaced them, and in their Prussian garrisons the Imam called the faithful to prayer. In 1807 at Eylau their lances repaid the Prussian King for his tolerance; soon after that they became the nucleus of the Uhlan regiments of the new Prussia.

The century of the 'cabinet war' was over. Soon the existence not merely of small states but of great nations would be at stake; and as the motives for war changed, so too did the face of war, and the appearance of the men who fought it.

The American War of Independence 1775-83

JOHN MOLLO

Twelve years after the Seven Years' War ended in 1763 the dispute between Great Britain and her North American colonies burst into open conflict. During the course of what was to become the American War of Independence, troops from various of the smaller German states, and from France, were involved in the fighting, and when the war ended in 1783 lessons learned in America were carried back to Europe to reappear six years later when the French had their own revolution.

The military lessons, learned at great cost by the British and the colonists during the so-called French and Indian War of 1754–60, were promptly forgotten by the former after the peace of 1763, and it was some time before the knowledge was regained.

As one of the bones of contention between Britain and the colonists concerned the cost of defence of the colonies, a short examination of the development of their land forces will not be out of place. The forces at the disposal of the North American colonies developed, from the end of the seventeenth century, into three categories. The first was the militia, organized by counties, which, apart from the Quakers of Pennsylvania, clergymen, university students and public officials, comprised all adult white males. They met at irregular periods for training and as the tension increased between the colonists and the mother country 'Alarm Companies' of 'Minutemen' were formed who could turn out fully armed and equipped at a moment's notice. It was these minutemen who were engaged in the opening action of the war at Lexington and Concord.

When major operations were undertaken, as in the past against the French and Indians, and now against the British, state regiments were raised from the militia 'for service'. These varied in size and length of service from campaign to campaign, but the usual commitment was for one year at the end of which attempts were made to retain the more seasoned men. The New England army, which was taken over at Cambridge as the first 'Continental' army, was formed from such provincial units, together with some of the third category of troops, the Volunteer Companies, which were raised from time to time in the more populated areas from the wealthier members of the militia, who drilled more often, wore uniform and maintained a unity and discipline quite foreign to the militia. Although nominally part of the militia they were, in effect, private military associations chartered and authorized to bear arms. The artillery of the New England army was largely composed of such private companies.

While this system worked well enough in the small-scale operations of the French and Indian Wars it was no match for the might of the regular British Army and it was soon apparent that a continental standing army was required. In July 1775 George Washington took over command of the New England army besieging Boston and early in the following year the first Continental regiments were raised and signed up for three years, or for the duration of the war. Thereafter the army remained steady at a strength of 15,000 to 17,000, except for the disastrous winter of 1777–8 at Valley Forge, when it was reduced to about 3,000 men. It was composed of infantry units with a small artillery corps and a sprinkling of cavalry.

After Valley Forge, when Washington's drill-master, the Prussian Baron von Steuben, introduced Prussian drill and proper discipline, the 'regular' army returned to its strength of 15,000 increasing each spring, on the eve of a new campaign, and

OPPOSITE 'George Washington at Princeton' by C. W. Peale. Washington, as commander of the New England Army, defeated the Hessians at Trenton on 29 December 1776 and the British at Princeton on 3 January 1777.

falling off again every autumn with the first snow. The militia was still used for the vital purpose of holding the countryside, while the regular army kept the British concentrated. After Valley Forge, through the influence of von Steuben, who had seen similar units in action during the Seven Years' War, so-called 'legions', small units of combined arms, usually of doubtful performance and reputation, appeared. In 1778 a light infantry company was added to every regiment. As was the custom at the time these were amalgamated on service and eventually the 2,000 strong Corps of Light Infantry was formed and commanded by the Marquis de Lafayette.

The clothing of the militia was essentially civilian, with the addition of musket, powder horn, bullet bag and tomahawk, and only the officers in some isolated cases appear to have worn uniform, usually a plain red coat, gorget and crimson sash. The states which sent units to the New England army made an attempt to provide them with uniform hats and coats in the traditional colours of brown or blue, while the waistcoats, breeches, stockings, shoes and other articles were of individual colour and pattern. Some frontier units, notably the Pennsylvania Rifle Regiment, wore 'Indian', or hunting dress, consisting of a fringed rifle smock, leggings and moccasins. This style of dress, which had been adopted early on by the French trappers, the *coureurs de bois*, and had been copied by the English frontiersmen, had many advocates among military men after the dismal defeat of a British force under General Braddock, in 1755, particularly in Virginia, where a Colonel Byrd was reported to have had 'most of his best people equipt in that manner'. Washington, who thought it cheap, clean, light and adaptable, requested 10,000 sets to be furnished for the Continental army. Congress included rifle

frocks in the clothing bounty given to the rank and file and states also supplied them to their own troops, as a working dress, or when coats were unobtainable, and their use became so general that to all intents and purposes they became the service dress of the American army and as such may be said to be North America's contribution to the development of military dress.

In November 1775 Congress adopted brown as the first official uniform colour of the Continental army, the various regiments being distinguished by different coloured collars, cuffs and lapels. The cut of the coats was similar to that of the British, but plainer and with worked instead of laced buttonholes. Cocked hats with a black cockade, white or buff waistcoats and breeches, stockings, shoes and half-spatterdashes completed the regulation dress; but, as some of the earlier units had already chosen their uniforms, brown was by no means universally adopted. In 1775 home industry was in its infancy and there were severe shortages of clothing, blankets, woollen and cotton goods, supplies of which were eked out by imports from France and thinly disguised captured British uniforms. Occasionally blue and brown broadcloth was purchased in Europe by American agents and shipped to North America, running the gauntlet of the Royal Navy. Washington hoped to have all the Continental army in uniform by the beginning of 1776, but he was only partially successful and those uniforms which were issued were very soon worn out in the trenches before New York.

.The pre-revolutionary marks of an officer, gorget, sash and espontoon, proved inadequate to protect the authority of the largely elected American officers, and in July 1775 an *ad hoc* system of rank badges was introduced. All general officers, brigade-majors and aides-de-camp were to have a broad ribbon across the breast, blue for the commander-in-chief, pink for major-generals and green for brigade-majors and aides-de-camp. Subsequently major-generals were given purple ribbons while brigadier-generals retained the pink. Field officers were to have pink cockades in their hats, captains yellow, changed in 1776 to white or buff, and subalterns green. Sergeants were to have a red epaulette or a strip of red cloth on the right shoulder and corporals the same in green.

In September 1778, 20,000 uniform suits in blue and brown faced with red were received from France and with these Washington managed to clothe his army during the winter of 1778–9. Early the following year he submitted a plan for clothing the army, in which he proposed a different colour for each state, with the state regiments distinguished by various colours and arrangements of facings, rather in the French style. He also proposed that breeches should be abolished in favour of overalls, wool in winter and linen in summer.

In May, the Board of War, to whom Congress had passed Washington's plans, countered with one of their own, in which all uniforms, with the exception of the waggoners who were to have brown or grey coats, were to be dark blue, with white linings and buttons, and white waistcoats and breeches. The final plan as approved by Washington divided the infantry into four groups of states, each with a different facing colour. Thus New Hampshire (NH), Massachusetts (MB), Rhode Island (RI), and Connecticut (C) had white facings and buttons marked with the initial letters of the states. New York (NY) and New Jersey (NJ) had buff facings, waistcoats and breeches, and yellow hat, lace and buttons. Pennsylvania (P), Delaware (D), Maryland (M) and Virginia (V) had red facings and white buttons.

Finally North Carolina (NC), South Carolina (SC) and Georgia (G) had blue facings with white laced buttonholes and white buttons.

The requirements of the Board of War were passed to the American minister at Versailles but there was only enough money to purchase 10,000 suits and 15,000 stand of arms and accoutrements, most of which did not arrive until late in 1780 and early in 1781. Washington published a condensed version of the Board's scheme in a General Order of 22 October 1779, but it is not clear to what extent the Continental army actually wore these new uniforms. The regulations, however, remained in force until December 1782, when the whole Continental infantry and cavalry were clothed in blue with red facings.

Under the new scheme the Continental light dragoons were to have blue uniforms, faced in white, and with blue epaulettes for the NCOs. The corps of light infantry wore their regimental uniforms, but with a light infantry cap decorated with a red and black plume. The artillery wore blue with red facings and yellow buttons and lace, and the engineer officers blue with buff facings and red linings. Drummers and fifers wore the reversed colours of their groups, except those of the last group, who wore dark blue with white lace trimming.

New rank markings were introduced in July 1780. General officers were to wear blue coats with buff facings, waistcoats and breeches and gold epaulettes and buttons. The commander-in-chief had three silver stars on each epaulette and a plain hat without a feather; major-generals two silver stars and a black and white feather; brigadier-generals one star and a white feather. Brigade-majors and aides-de-camp wore the uniform of their corps. Field-officers had two epaulettes, captains one on the right shoulder and subalterns one on

OVERPAGE 'Warley Camp' by De Loutherberg. This painting is one of a pair showing incidents from the militia camp held on Warley Common in 1778. The scene shows a mock attack by light infantry and grenadiers, part of a review held before George III.

'Captain and Lieutenant-Colonel The Hon. Cosmo Gordon' attributed to Francis Wheatley. The second son of the Earl of Aberdeen, Cosmo Gordon served in America as an officer of grenadiers in the 3rd Foot Guards. He was promoted to captain and lieutenant-colonel in 1773, and this portrait shows him in the uniform he would have worn in the war.

the left. Sergeants had two silk epaulettes in the button colour, except for the light dragoons, and corporals two in worsted. In July 1780 a white centre was added to the black hat cockade, as a reciprocal gesture to the French who, on their arrival in North America, had paid the compliment of mounting a black cockade over the white cockade of the Bourbons.

The bulk of the American infantry was armed with smoothbore flintlock muskets, several different types and calibres, including French, Dutch and even Prussian models, being in use at the same time. At Valley Forge muskets, carbines, fowling pieces and rifles could often be found in the same company. The reputation of the American rifle, introduced in 1700 by German and Swiss emigrants, has been much exaggerated; they were few in number, slow to load, unreliable in bad weather, could not be fitted with a bayonet and thus could not be used in the battle line. The number of rifles was gradually reduced until, by 1781, they were 'generally disused'.

Each soldier carried some thirty rounds made up into cartridges, but there was a shortage of cartouche boxes, and at one stage Washington introduced tin canisters to contain them. Bayonets often had to be made individually to fit the wide assortment of weapons in use, and although unpopular at first, were used to great effect at Stony Point in 1779, and at Yorktown. Officers, up to and including the rank of captain, carried swords and espontoons, light infantry subalterns carrying light muskets or 'fusils'. Sergeants were armed with muskets and bayonets, and occasionally with a short sword, or hanger, in addition.

Opposed to the colonists was the regular British army of 48,000 men, of whom only 8,000 men were stationed in North America at the outbreak of the war. With her world-wide commitments Britain had difficulty in assembling enough troops to quell the disturbances of April 1775, and was forced to call in the help of foreign mercenaries. From the beginning of the war until the surrender of Burgoyne's 5,000 strong army at Saratoga in October 1777, only one new regiment was added to the army; but after Saratoga, fear of a French invasion, and reforms in the recruiting laws, improved the situation so that by the end of the war the army had increased to 110,000 men, of whom some 56,000 saw service in America.

The main battle line of the army consisted of the regiments of infantry, of one or two battalions, of 477 men each. The service battalion was divided into ten companies, one of which was the 'grenadier', and another the 'light infantry' company. The former, whose original task had been to hurl hand-grenades, consisted of the 'tallest and briskest fellows', and the latter of good marksmen of light build and active temperament. From their 'posts of honour' on the right and left flanks of the battalion, these picked men became known as the 'flank companies', and the remaining eight as the 'battalion companies'. Only two cavalry regiments, the 16th and 17th Light Dragoons, served in America, but there were several companies of Royal Artillery in attendance to serve the guns that accompanied the army in the field.

The first regulation dress for field-marshals and general officers appeared in 1767. Their everyday, or frock, uniform consisted of a red coat with blue collar patches, lapels and cuffs, gold buttons and embroidered holes, white waistcoat and breeches, crimson waist sash, and black boots. Generals had their buttonholes placed regularly, lieutenant-generals in threes, and major-generals in pairs. All had two blue epaulettes embroidered in gold. Staff officers were rather more vaguely

described, but by 1775 they were wearing red coats with blue collars, cuffs and lapels. Adjutant and quartermaster-generals had two silver epaulettes and silver laced holes, set in threes. Their deputies had their laced holes in pairs and if attached to an infantry formation, a single epaulette on the right shoulder, if to a cavalry formation, one on the left. Aides-de-camp had gold epaulettes and laced buttonholes set regularly and brigade-majors the same but in silver.

The infantry were dressed in accordance with the royal warrant of 1768, which had confirmed various stylistic changes inspired by the Prussian army. Thus the coat was made shorter and tighter, and the former red or blue waistcoat and breeches changed for white or buff. The old cloth mitre grenadier caps were replaced by fur caps, said to have been based on those of the French grenadiers captured at Wilhelmstal in 1762. The battalion companies wore large black cocked hats, coarse red coats, with regimentally coloured collars, cuffs and lapels, trimmed with variously coloured regimental braid, white or buff waistcoat and breeches, stockings, knee-length black gaiters and shoes. The knapsack, blanket, haversack containing four days' provisions, water flask, cartouche box containing sixty rounds and weapons completed a load of some sixty pounds. Apart from their caps, which now had a japanned metal plate in the front bearing the King's crest and the motto *nec aspera terrent*, the grenadiers were further distinguished by the cloth 'wings' on their shoulders and the brass match-cases on their cartouche belts.

The distinctive dress of the light infantry company attached to each battalion in 1771 was developed during the fighting against the French in Canada, during the Seven Years' War, temporarily falling into disuse after 1763. The essential differences were the cap, of which a bewildering variety

GREAT BRITAIN

Sergeant of the 47th Regiment of Foot

Infantryman of the 9th Regiment of Foot

Officer of the 5th Infantry Regiment

Grenadier Officer of the 37th Regiment of Foot

Musketeer of the 1st Regiment of Foot Guards

GREAT BRITAIN

Rifleman of the North Carolina Volunteers

Infantryman of the King's Royal Regiment of New York, 1776–7

Officer of the 17th Light Dragoon Regiment, 1776

Gunner of the Royal Regiment of Artillery, 1776

Officer of the Light Infantry, 1777–8

AMERICA

Infantryman of the North Carolina Regiments, 1779

Infantryman of Colonel Webb's Regiment, 1777

Infantryman of the New Jersey Infantry, 1780

Infantryman of the 12th Regiment of the Continental Army, 1778

Officer of the 8th Regiment of the Continental Army, 1776

AMERICA

Officer of the 2nd Regiment of Continental Light Dragoons, 1779

Artilleryman of the Continental Artillery Corps, 1780

Brigadier-General, 1780

Officer of the Engineer Corps, 1780

Corporal of Colonel Hartley's Regiment, 1777

existed according to regiment, the retention of the recently discarded red waistcoat and the half-spatterdashes which were quickly adopted by the whole infantry. In addition, the light infantry wore pouches on a waist-belt at the front, and carried powder-horns and tomahawks as well as bayonets. The light infantry companies in North America were formed into battalions and it appears that some form of field-sign, a dark armband for instance, was adopted by the officers to distinguish the battalions. Three regiments, the 7th, 21st, and 23rd, were designated 'fusiliers', a form of infantry introduced into the British army by the Duke of Marlborough in 1702, for the purpose of protecting the train of artillery. Although no longer carrying out this role, they were distinguished by the whole regiment being dressed as grenadiers, but with slightly lower caps.

Regimental officers were chiefly distinguished by their gorgets and crimson waist-sashes, but an embryo system of rank markings was coming into use whereby field-officers and officers of grenadiers wore two epaulettes, and captains and subalterns one only on the right shoulder.

Drummers and fifers wore coats of the facing colour, except for those of 'royal' regiments, who wore red, faced and lapelled in blue, and of regiments with red facings, who wore white, faced and lapelled in red. Their caps were of black bearskin, with the 'King's Crest, of Silver-plated Metal, on a Black Ground, with Trophies of Colours and Drums' [Royal Warrant, 1751]. The number of the regiment appeared on the back. They were armed with short swords with a scimitar blade.

In every infantry battalion ten men, under the command of a corporal, were appointed to act as pioneers carrying out minor engineering tasks. They wore low black fur caps with a red lacquered front

'The Surrender of Burgoyne'. Major-General John Burgoyne arrived from Britain at the outbreak of the Revolution. He was defeated at the Battle of Saratoga in 1777.

plate, with the king's arms and a crossed saw and axe, in silver. In addition they wore leather aprons and carried various tools.

Three regiments, the 42nd, 71st and 76th wore Scottish, or 'Highland Dress'. This consisted of a flat blue bonnet with a red, white and green 'diced' band, a bunch of feathers at the side, short red jacket, white waistcoat, belted plaid in the regiment's tartan, sporran, diced hose and light shoes.

As the war progressed alterations were made to the basic dress of the infantry to meet combat conditions. Firstly half-spatterdashes were adopted by all companies and then the waist-belt which carried the bayonet began to be worn over the right shoulder. Gradually proper shoulder-belts, with regimental clasps, were introduced. When a 'brigade' of footguards from the three regiments was sent to America in 1776, the officers and sergeants were allowed to wear white lace, like the men, instead of gold, and they carried fusils. During the Pennsylvania campaign of 1777-8 a new form of dress appears in contemporary watercolours by Xavier Gatta. Battalion company men of the 40th regiment are shown in slouched hats with a red feather, plain red single-breasted sleeved waist-coats, white breeches and stockings and half-spatterdashes. Men of the 2nd battalion of light infantry wear a similar uniform, but with a black hat feather, black equipment and white overalls. Short single-breasted jackets with collars and pointed cuffs of regimental facing colours became very popular during the second half of the war, particularly for British and American cavalry units. During Burgoyne's ill-fated expedition another modified uniform appeared. The commanding officers of the regiments taking part were ordered to cut down their coats and to convert their hats into caps with a horsehair crest of different regimental colours. During the closing

GERMAN STATES
Hessen-Kassel, Musketeer of von Trümbach's Infantry Regiment, 1776

Hessen-Hanau, Grenadier of the Crown Prince's Infantry Regiment, 1776

Anspach-Bayreuth, Grenadier Sergeant of the 2nd Infantry Regiment, 1777

Hessen-Kassel, Gunner of the Artillery Company, 1776

Hessen-Kassel, Chasseur, 1777

GERMAN STATES
Anhalt-Zerbst, Infantryman, 1777–8

Brunswick, Infantryman of Prince Frederick's Infantry Regiment, 1776

Brunswick, Dragoon of Prince Ludwig's Regiment, 1777

Brunswick, Chasseur, 1776

Waldeck, Infantryman, 1776

FRANCE
Saintonge Infantry
Regiment, 1780

Officer of the Bourbon
Infantry Regiment, 1780

Grenadier Officer of the
Royal Deux-Ponts
(Zweibrücken) Regiment,
1780

Officer of the Agenois
Infantry Regiment, 1780

Gatenois Infantry
Regiment, 1780

FRANCE
Gunner of the Royal
Artillery Corps, 1780

Hussar of the Lauzun
Legion, 1780

General's Adjutant in gala
uniform, 1780

Officer of the Royal
Marine Infantry Corps,
1780

Grenadier of the Lauzun
Legion, 1780

stages of the war in the south it appears that the troops taking part may have worn white jackets, possibly sleeved waistcoats and white broad-brimmed hats.

The two light dragoon regiments wore special helmets, red coats, white waistcoats and breeches and black boots. The 16th light dragoons had blue facings and the 17th white. The Royal Artillery wore blue coats with red facings, yellow buttons and lace, white waistcoats and breeches, gaiters and shoes. During Burgoyne's expedition, like the rest of the army, they wore short jackets and a cap with a red crest.

The British infantryman was armed with the famous 'Brown Bess' flintlock musket which had been in service since 1717. Reliable enough, except in bad weather, it was not much use beyond eighty yards' range. Twelve separate movements were needed to prime and load this cumbersome weapon; nevertheless a trained soldier could loose off five one-ounce lead balls a minute. It was equipped with a socket bayonet with a triangular section blade. The cavalry were armed with flintlock carbines, pistols and swords.

Some 19,000 'loyalists' fought on the British side, forming forty-one regiments, comprising some 300 provincial companies. Alongside the familiar regiments, the Royal Americans, Butler's Rangers and the King's Royal Regiment, there were numerous units with more exotic titles. Two loyalist regiments became regular units of the army, the Royal Highland Emigrants and the Volunteers of Ireland.

The majority of the provincial corps consisted of line infantry, with the usual grenadier and light infantry, rangers and light dragoons, who were in some cases formed into legions of horse and foot. At first there were no uniforms; the earliest Boston units, for example, wore civilian clothing, distinguished by such field-signs as cockades

and armbands. After the British capture of New York, in 1776, bulk clothing for the use of the provincials was sent out from England, and by the spring of 1778 some 10,000 suits of green regimentals with white buttons and red, white or blue facings had been supplied. With them came white waistcoats and breeches, dark brown gaiters, hats and accoutrements of standard British design. The weapons were the same as those issued to the regulars, although in many cases the provincials were issued with the older 'Long Land' pattern of 'Brown Bess'.

In 1778 it was decided to clothe the provincials in red and further supplies were sent out with white, buff, orange, blue, green or black facings. Waistcoats and breeches were white except for those regiments with buff facings. Henceforth the custom seems to have been adopted of buying up clothing left in store by returning British regiments, and the uniforms of the 10th, 46th and 52nd regiments all passed into provincial service in this way. While the majority of colonels seemed happy at the change, some, like Colonel Simcoe of the Queen's Rangers, fought hard to keep their green clothing. The light dragoons were at first dressed in red, but later some regiments were ordered into green, so that they could serve with the Queen's Rangers. Banastre Tarleton's British Legion, which acquired a fierce reputation in the southern fighting, also wore green. Portraits of Tarleton and George Hanger, also of the British Legion, show them wearing the fur-crested helmet later adopted by the British regular light dragoons and known as the 'Tarleton helmet'.

During the last two years of the war in the south the provincials came into their own, but though their role in battle was slight, loyalists played a key part in the underground world of the spy and the informer.

'General Sir Banastre Tarleton 1754–1833' by Sir Joshua Reynolds. The man the rebels called 'Bloody Tarleton' is pictured here as a young cavalry officer, a lieutenant-colonel at twenty-six, wearing the uniform of the British Legion, a unit of American Loyalist cavalry.

'The Siege of Yorktown' by
Van Blarenbergue, 16–19
October 1781. Between
double ranks of allied
troops Cornwallis's army,
smartly dressed in new
uniforms but with Colours
cased, marches along the
York–Hampton road to lay
down their arms.

Britain's mistake, in her handling of the loyalist situation, was turning to them for assistance too late, and then after Saratoga, placing too much reliance on them.

In addition to the loyalists, the British had the dubious assistance of some 1,000 Red Indians. The bulk of these were Iroquois from the Mohawk valley, who had been administered for the previous twenty years by Sir William Johnson, the 'Superintendent of the Northern Indians'. After his death in 1774, his son, Sir John, and his nephew, Guy, kept at least four of the 'Six Nations' on the British side. Throughout the war the Mohawks led by Joseph Brant proved troublesome allies, their savage raids causing a loss of goodwill towards the British; nevertheless they were active, if barbarous, fighters and stood by Britain throughout the war.

The Indians wore hunting shirts, leggings and deerskin moccasins, frequently made of red or blue 'trader's' cloth, decorated with beads and porcupine quills. Chiefs sometimes adopted British officers' gorgets and sashes. Most warriors shaved their heads, cutting the hair as close to head as possible, except for a long braided 'scalp lock', growing out of the crown, to which a crest of deer tails, moose hair, turkey feathers and porcupine quills, was attached. The crest and a large part of the head were dyed vermilion, the most popular colour for the ceremonial warpaint, although charcoal, ochre and vegetable green were also used. The importance of Indian dress in influencing the development of light infantry and rangers in the British army and the dress of the American frontiersman has already been mentioned.

Until they were supplied with firearms, the Iroquois were mainly armed with the war club, the tomahawk, the bow and occasionally a short lance and shield; in addition every brave carried a scalping knife. In the early colonial period vigorous attempts were made to prevent the Indians obtaining firearms, but by various means, both legal and illegal, they managed to acquire them. The firearm soon became an object of status and Indians were prepared to pay vast sums for a weapon, usually calculated in piles of beaver skins.

In 1776, the first full year of the war, some 20,000 German auxiliary troops arrived to help the British in North America. The strength of this force, which almost equalled that of the regular British forces in America, remained constant throughout the war. Further treaties were made from time to time for additional companies of *Jägers* who were found to be particularly useful in America.

The two largest contingents, from Hessen-Kassel and Brunswick, were similar in appearance, if not in quality. The Hessen-Kassel soldiers were largely regulars, many of whom had seen service in the Seven Years' War, and their officers were career soldiers. The uniforms of the Hessen-Kassel infantry were similar to those of the Prussian army and were of similar coarse and cheap material. They were too hot in summer and too cold in winter, and there were no greatcoats, except for a few watchcoats kept for the use of sentries. The infantry wore medium blue coats with lapels and Prussian cuffs of regimental colours, white, yellow or 'straw' waistcoats and breeches, black gaiters and shoes. The battalion company men, known as musketeers, wore cocked hats garnished with worsted pom-poms and tassels, while the grenadiers and fusiliers wore special Prussian-style mitre caps, with metal fronts emblazoned with various heraldic devices.

The equipment of the men consisted of a large fur knapsack slung over one shoulder, together with a large tin water flask on a buff leather strap. Over the other shoulder went a broad buff leather belt, which supported the black leather cartouche box, which was decorated with a brass or white metal plate.

The officers had ornamental buttonholes on their coats, gorgets and silver net waist-sashes with two large hanging tassels, but as the war progressed the embroidery was removed and the officers were ordered to dress like their men and to carry fusils instead of espontoons. The Hessian officers, at the beginning of the New York campaign, marched on foot, with their cloaks rolled about them, each with a large, gourd-shaped flask of rum and water at his side. Many of them slung their fusils during the march, and even the field officers could be seen taking part in the firing during an action. After the first engagement the men were allowed to wear their waist-belts over their shoulders.

The *Jägers*, recruited from huntsmen and foresters, wore green uniforms with crimson facings, similar to those of the Prussian *Feldjäger* corps, the officers wearing gold shoulder cords, and the sergeants having their coats edged with gold lace. The cartouche pouches, worn at the waist in front, bore the crown and cipher CFCA in yellow metal. Their rifles, often the private property of the men, were outmoded and inferior to those carried by the American marksmen. The *Jägers* were a mounted unit but left their horses and saddlery at home.

The Brunswick troops were dressed in blue, like the Hessians, but in 'old and bad clothing'. The cut was tight and skimpy and the facings, collars and cuffs were mere strips of coloured cloth sewn on to the coats, with cheap, plain buttons. In fact their clothing was so bad that the British government had to advance General von Riedesel £5,000 to dress his men properly. An inspecting officer at Stade noted that the Brunswickers were 'far from making a fine body of men, having a greater number of small and ill-looking and many old people among them'. The Brunswick infantry uniforms differed from those of the Hessians, having only four buttons, in pairs, on the lapels and 'Swedish' cuffs with two buttons. The musicians generally wore yellow coats.

The Brunswick *Jägers* had green coats with red lapels, Swedish cuffs and linings, yellow buttons and shoulder-knots, green waistcoats, straw breeches, black gaiters and shoes. The dragoon regiment, Prince Ludwig, which, like the Hessian *Jägers*, served dismounted, had light blue coats, like the Prussian dragoons, eminently unsuitable for forest fighting, yellow facings and waistcoats, white buttons and shoulder-knots, buff breeches, marching gaiters and shoes. The Brunswick contingent took part in Burgoyne's expedition and after the surrender at Saratoga ceased to exist as a fighting unit.

In addition to these larger units there were smaller detachments from Hesse-Hanau, Waldeck, Anspach-Bayreuth and Anhalt-Zerbst. The first of these provided one infantry regiment and an artillery company, both dressed in blue with red facings, after the Prussian style. Waldeck provided a regiment of infantry and a small train of artillery, dressed in blue with yellow facings and white buttons, white waistcoats and breeches. Their grenadiers wore Austrian-style fur caps, without plates but with yellow cloth bags, trimmed with white lace and finished off with a white tassel. Anspach-Bayreuth provided two Brandenburg-Anspach infantry regiments, an Anspach-Bayreuth *Jäger* company and an artillery company. The infantry wore blue; the 1st regiment with red facings and the 2nd with black, the grenadiers having fur caps with a silver plate and red bag. The artillery wore blue with crimson facings and the *Jägers* green with crimson facings, green waistcoats and buff breeches. Anhalt-Zerbst sent one infantry regiment of two battalions, dressed in white with red lapels, Swedish cuffs and linings, and yellow buttons. A second contingent, which arrived in New York in August 1781, wore a curious hussar-like uniform with a cylindrical felt shako, Hungarian boots and a red cloak, the whole effect being rather like the Austrian Pandours and Croats.

Between a third and a half of the German troops sent to America failed to return to their native lands, a great proportion of them remaining in America as settlers. Although at first they were feared by the local population, the 'Hessians', as the German auxiliaries were collectively known, were certainly not the ogres they have been painted, and as the war progressed were generally better liked and more civilly treated than the British. When taken prisoner both officers and men were shown favours never bestowed on their British comrades, in order to persuade them to desert after they were exchanged.

The German officers who returned home took back with them valuable experience gained in America. In the wars that followed the French Revolution the German leaders trained in the school of Frederick the Great were too old for active service and their place was taken by many who had seen service in America. Indeed a Prussian general of the time asserted that, of all the troops fighting France during the campaign of 1792–4, those of Hessen-Kassel were the best.

Until the surrender of Burgoyne's force at Saratoga, France was content to interfere only indirectly in what was a domestic issue between Great Britain and the colonists. The rebels needed powder and other supplies and assistance against the British naval supremacy, which blocked the free move-

Benedict Arnold, the hero of the Battle of Saratoga, is unhorsed as the Americans encounter a group of Major-General von Riedesel's Hessians.

ment of troops and supplies along the Atlantic seaboard. In February 1778, after months of deliberation, France signed a treaty of friendship and commerce with the 'United States of North America', which soon led to a state of war between Great Britain and France.

In July 1780 a French force under the command of the Comte de Rochambeau arrived at Newport, Rhode Island, where it remained throughout the winter, depriving the British forces in New York of their freedom of action. In the spring of 1781 Rochambeau joined Washington on the Hudson and the combined force, marching rapidly through New Jersey, Pennsylvania and Delaware, succeeded in bottling the British up in Yorktown, Virginia. After a resistance of thirteen days the British under Cornwallis surrendered, effectively bringing the war to an end.

Rochambeau's original force of some 8,000 men was reinforced, before Yorktown, by 3,000 men from the West Indies, under the command of Saint-Simon. The combined army consisted of six French and one German infantry regiment, artillery and Lauzun's Legion, the hussars which were the only French mounted troops serving in America, although some 'dragoons' or 'hussars' are said to have accompanied Saint-Simon's force.

The large staff of this army was clothed in accordance with the regulations of September 1775. The everyday uniform of the general officers consisted of a blue coat, embroidered with a gold wave pattern, white waistcoat and breeches, and boots. Aides-de-camp wore epaulettes of their rank and a blue single-breasted coat, with gold-embroidered edges and loops, eight down each front, two on each cuff and three on each pocket flap. The War Commissar and his assistants, who combined the duties of the British and American adjutants and quartermaster-generals, wore gold-embroidered grey coats, and red waistcoats, breeches and stockings.

The French infantry regiments wore cocked hats and coats, waistcoats and breeches of the traditional greyish-white cloth, the colour of undyed wool. The German infantry regiment Deuxponts, and the infantry of Lauzun's Legion wore coats of sky-blue with yellow facings. The various regiments were distinguished by the colour of the collars, lapels and cuffs and the arrangement of the buttons, and by various shapes of coat pocket flap. White gaiters were worn in summer and black in winter. In 1763, after the Seven Years' War, a new uniform was introduced, based on the Prussian model, with a tight coat and small false cuffs and pocket flaps. It is thought that Rochambeau's corps wore the uniforms of the 1767 pattern, as they left France too soon to have received the new uniforms according to the regulations of 21 February 1779, and that Saint-Simon's corps were probably wearing the new pattern.

Under the 1767 regulations regiments were distinguished by their numbered buttons, in white or yellow metal, and the colour of their cuffs, lapels and piping. Fusiliers had their hats bordered in white or yellow lace, according to their buttons. From 1767 to 1775 many styles of head-dress were tried out in the French army; large hats, small hats, boiled leather caps, metal helmets, black leather helmets and fur grenadier caps, were all tried and eventually abandoned. There is evidence, however, that one regiment, Soissonois, was still wearing fur grenadier caps, officially abolished in 1779, when it marched through Philadelphia on its way to Yorktown. The crested helmets adopted by some regiments after 1772 were abolished in May 1776, but as they were to be kept until they wore out, it is possible,

but as yet unproven, that some of Rochambeau's regiments wore them.

Officers wore similar uniforms to their men's, but made of better quality stuff. Their rank was indicated by their gilt gorgets and their gold or silver epaulettes, the arrangement of which was the most sophisticated system of rank markings yet in existence. Colonels had two epaulettes with bullion fringe and lieutenant-colonels one similar on the left shoulder. Majors had two

epaulettes with twist fringe, and captains one similar on the left shoulder. Lieutenants had one epaulette on the left shoulder with the strap of metal lace woven with a coloured lozenge pattern and mixed metal and coloured silk fringe, and sub-lieutenants had the same but in reversed colours, that is, a coloured strap woven with a metal lozenge pattern. Officers with one epaulette only wore a *contre-epaulette* on the right shoulder, which consisted of the

'Washington and his generals at Yorktown' by James Peale. Washington is seen, after the British capitulation, on the shore of the York river at the western end of Yorktown. British ships are sunk in the water and horses lie dead on the beach.

epaulette strap without any fringe. Sergeants were distinguished by a row of silver lace round the cuffs, and corporals by two rows of blue braid.

By the 1779 Regulations, the French infantry, with the exception of the Royal regiments, the regiments of the Princes and the Picardie regiment, were divided into ten groups of six regiments, each group or division having its own distinguishing colour, as follows:

Regiments	Colours
1–6	Sky-blue
7–12	Black
15–19	Violet
20–27	Steel-grey
28–34	Rose
35–40	Primrose
41–51	Crimson
52–62	Silver-grey
70–72	Aurora
82–94	Dark green

Each division was divided into two groups of three regiments, one with yellow buttons and horizontal pocket flaps and the other with white buttons and vertical pocket flaps. The three regiments in each group were further distinguished by differences in the cuffs and lapels. Thus, the first regiment had lapels and cuffs of the group colour, the second lapels and cuff piping only and the third cuffs and lapel piping only. The pocket flaps in all cases were piped in the group colour. This system, which exceeds anything dreamed up by the Prussians shows the lengths to which the mania for uniformity led the admirers of Frederick the Great.

By the regulations of 1779 the battalion companies, or fusiliers, wore hats without lace but with a white cockade, white shoulder straps piped in the group colour and cloth skirt ornaments in the group colour, cut in the shape of a *fleur-de-lys*.

The grenadiers had hats with red pom-poms, red shoulder straps piped in white and cloth grenades on the skirts. The light infantry, or chasseurs, had hats with a green cockade, green shoulder straps piped in white and a cloth bugle horn on the skirts.

After 1767 there were various equipment changes, the most drastic of which was the abolition of the waist-belt, the bayonet being henceforth carried in a frog attached to the cartouche belt. Grenadiers, however, were in 1770 given curved *sabre-briquets*, and so wore a second crossbelt in which it was carried. A fur-covered knapsack, a large linen haversack, in which the soldier could wrap himself at night, and a gourd-shaped water flask completed the field equipment.

The infantry weapon was the flintlock musket and bayonet, the first model of which had appeared in 1717. The 1746, and subsequent, models were equipped with iron ramrods and other improvements were incorporated in the models of 1763, 1766, 1770, 1771 and 1774. After 1766 officers were armed with fusils, bayonets, swords and cartouche boxes.

The artillery were dressed like the infantry, but in blue with red facings and blue waistcoats and breeches; they were armed with the shorter, artillery, version of the infantry musket. The hussars of Lauzun's Legion wore sky-blue jackets and pelisses, yellow facings and breeches, black felt *mirlitons* and black hussar boots.

The French experience in America, short as it was, exerted a lasting influence on the French army. The activities of Lafayette in the French Revolution are well known. What is perhaps less well known is that Napoleon's chief of staff, Berthier, was one of Rochambeau's aides-de-camp, and that Du Portail, who as Minister of War was responsible for a later reorganization of the French army, also served in America.

Wars of the French Revolution and the Coalitions 1792-1803

3

PAUL MARTIN

The experience gained during the American War of Independence was to play an important part in the strategy, organization, armament and uniform of the French and British armies in the late eighteenth century. In France, two names in particular are significant in connection with subsequent reforms: Lafayette and the war minister Du Portail, both former aides-de-camp of Rochambeau. In France, military organization, and especially matters of clothing and arms, was governed by the ordinances of 1786 and 1790. The cut and manufacture of uniforms generally followed the tight impractical fashions of the day, as did head-dress and hair style.

At the moment when rumours of mutiny at Metz and Nancy were heralding the momentous events of 1789, the French army consisted of the troops of the *Maison du Roi* (horse and foot guards), French and foreign infantry regiments of the line, heavy cavalry, dragoons, *chasseurs à cheval*, hussars and artillery. With the exception of the guards, the French infantry wore white, while of the foreign regiments in French service the Swiss wore red, the Germans pale blue and the Irish red. The heavy cavalry included only one regiment of cuirassiers, which wore iron breast-plates. The other regiments wore blue coats, the dragoons and chasseurs green. The mounted *grenadiers à cheval* and carabiniers had fur caps, while the dragoons wore crested helmets. The hussars dressed in the Hungarian style, in dolmans and pelisses, trimmed with coloured cord.

In Paris the ferment of 14 July 1789, when the French Guards and the people united to storm the Bastille, was the prelude to the great upheavals of the Revolution. Faced with the threat presented by the King's call for support from the foreign regiments, the bourgeoisie formed the National Guard and introduced with it an appropriate uniform, royal blue coats, white lapels and turnbacks, red collar and cuffs, whose tricolour theme echoed the national cockade and set the keynote for the great period to come. Soon the National Guard, both foot and horse, was organized on a national basis.

After 1792 the regular army was thrown into disarray by the emigration of officers and NCOs, and was soon in a sorry state. The revolutionary new concept of 'the fatherland in danger' saw the birth of the 'volunteers of the year I', amalgamated with the old troops of the *ancien régime*, making necessary the provision of makeshift clothing and equipment for the *levée en masse* of 1793. The *Maison du Roi* was abolished, the foreign regiments disbanded or transformed, the Swiss guards, loyal to the King, massacred in Paris on 10 August 1792, and the French Guards reorganized. The influx of young troops, mainly infantry, raised by the great organizer, Lazare Carnot led to rivalry between the battle-hardened veteran 'white coats' and the raw volunteer 'blue coats' of the 'nation in arms'.

The upheavals of the Revolution were to have extensive repercussions as the old world of elegant, sophisticated fashions, with its colourful military uniforms, gave way to a new era. The royal emblem, the *fleur-de-lys*, disappeared from flags and uniforms to be replaced by the lictor's *fasces*, surmounted by the red Phrygian cap of the Revolution. The knee-length breeches of the aristocrat gave way to the long striped trousers of the revolutionary. In the absence of muskets or sabres, the poorly armed infantry were issued with hurriedly forged pikes. They marched weighed down by a motley collection of utensils, underclothing, shoes, gaiters, mess tins, cooking pots and other possessions, fork

Soldiers of the French
infantry carrying a wounded
officer off the field.
Engraving by J. B. Seele.

A bivouac of a French infantry *de ligne* and light infantry showing the varied and ragged uniforms worn by the French troops. Engraving by Rugondas.

and spoon proudly thrust under the loop of the tricorn hat, a hunk of bread spitted on the end of the bayonet.

The battles of Valmy and Jemappes in 1792 brought appreciable losses of arms and equipment which made improvisation essential, especially in occupied enemy territory. So the *sans-culottes* shook the world by routing Prussian, Austrian and allied armies used to an outdated spit-and-polish concept of war. Freshly created *demibrigades* replaced the regiments of the *ancien régime*, and were led by bold generals proudly wearing the embroidered coat, plume and tricolour sash, among

whom Hoche, Kellerman, Kleber, and soon Bonaparte, were to go down in history. By virtue of his brilliant Italian campaign of 1796, conducted with ragged barefoot troops, the latter emerged as a great war leader.

The ordinary soldiers of the time – infantry, cavalry and artillery alike – affected the most unlikely and outlandish clothing, whose odd appearance has come down to us thanks to such painters as Albrecht Adam, Jean-Baptiste Seele and Benjamin Zix. They had no cloak or greatcoat during the winter months, acquiring such necessities from the local population. Often without

Napoleon in the military uniform of the *chasseur de la garde*. Painting by R. Lefebvre.

shoes and stockings, and with more and more makeshift equipment, they nevertheless knew how to march and how to fight. And the devotion of their brave women, *vivandières* or *cantinières*, in their semi-military dress, softened many of the hardships of war.

In place of the big regulation tricorn hat worn by the infantry and heavy cavalry, some infantry units had adopted a crested helmet, while both the mounted and dismounted grenadiers and carabiniers retained the traditional fur bonnet of the *corps d'élite*. The hussars kept their *mirlitons*, the peakless shako with a coloured cloth wing traditional among all the light cavalry in the armies of the time.

The National Convention was already under the protection of a guard whose uniform was based on that of the National Guard. In 1795 Bonaparte turned it into the Directory Guard, and in 1799 into the Consular Guard, which was the nucleus of the future Imperial Guard of Napoleon. From the start, the uniforms of these infantry and cavalry units were designed with special care, and the *têtes de colonne* were particularly well turned out.

For regiments of the line, the appearance around 1800 of the straight shako, with cords and a moveable peak, in the light infantry spread to the light cavalry and hussars. Later, around 1807, it replaced the tricorne of the *ancien régime* in all arms and units.

The musicians, hired instrumentalists of the band and the drummers and fifers of the *clique*, headed by a dashing drum-major, forming the *tête de colonne*, received special treatment and were distinctively dressed, often in the reversed colours of their units, with lavish braiding on the coat and sleeves. Some of these soon became the pride of their units, at the expense of the clothing regulations in force at the time.

The artillery still wore their traditional blue with red distinctions, and used the weapons developed under the Gribeauval system. Bonaparte gave this service his special attention, and it was he who created the light horse-drawn batteries of the Consular Guard, which wore the distinctive blue and red hussar-style uniform immortalized by General Baron Lejeune in his masterly painting of the battle of Marengo in 1803, now at Versailles. Lejeune was interested in the different uniforms and equipment of his time even before then, judging by the drawings and paintings which have come down to us as the most exact records of their day. These documents bear comparison with those of contemporary artists such as Carle Vernet, Duplessis-Bertaux and Schwebach or the drawings of the Consular Guard by Nicolas Hoffman.

Although Bonaparte dressed soberly himself, he had a feeling for pomp and ceremony, and already as First Consul was fond of surrounding himself with a General Staff clad in richly embroidered uniforms, particularly when reviewing the various regiments of the Consular Guard, the foot and horse grenadiers, mounted chasseurs and his beloved artillery. Impeccably turned out on parade, these hand-picked troops were also impressive in battle.

Already there was a tendency towards the deliberate development of special campaign clothing – a battledress for the time. The French armies fought in all kinds of more or less distant regions subject to very different seasons and climates – the Vendée, the Rhine, Flanders, the Netherlands (with the capture of the Dutch fleet at the Texel by a hussar regiment), southern Germany, Italy and even Egypt. The problem of supply was only one of the factors leading to departures from the strict letter of the clothing regulations.

The mid-1790s saw the appearance of the single-breasted coat as an undress, gradually replacing the old cut-away uniform with lapels. In the same period the cavalry were issued with long buttoned overalls, reinforced with leather, worn to protect the linen or leather breeches worn mainly by the hussars and mounted chasseurs. In Egypt the army had to resort to local materials, in whatever colours they could find, to clothe the army of occupation which confronted the local Mamelukes and the British in 1798.

Certainly the French had a tendency to treat the clothing regulations of the day with a lassitude, amounting almost to a native *fantaisie*, in the decoration or transformation of various details, already observable among the officers of the General Staff and extending to the *têtes de colonne* and musicians, whose expensive dress had to be paid for by the regiment and its colonel. For his own part the First Consul preferred to preach simplicity. He himself wore the undress coat of the *chasseurs à cheval* of his own guard and contented himself with a simple gold lace border to the tricorn hat which he was soon to abandon for the celebrated *petit chapeau*.

After the Italian campaign French uniform in general gave an ordered, even a dashing impression, to which the inhabitants and especially the female population of the invaded and occupied countries were not unsusceptible. Thus the French army, born under the Revolution and tempered by its various campaigns, and with pride in its arms and uniforms, could embark after 1803 upon the epic Imperial venture which was to set Europe ablaze.

It was the Emperor Napoleon himself who showed an expert's understanding of the value of military display when he said: 'The soldier must love his calling, and must find in it an outlet for his own enthusiasms

A French hussar and a standard-bearer around 1800 from an engraving by Carle Vernet.

and his sense of honour, which is why handsome uniforms are so useful – blue is the best colour, besides being the one by which we are known in Europe. Moreover coats must be comfortable and well made, and the soldier properly clad.'

The execution of Louis XVI in 1793 had stirred up a 'Holy Alliance' against France, a coalition of states made up of the Austria of Emperor Francis II, the nations of southern Germany, supported by the army of the French *émigrés*, the Prussia of Frederick William III, and subsequently Great Britain and Russia.

With the death of Frederick the Great in 1786 Prussia found herself in possession of a magnificent army which was bequeathed to his nephew, Frederick William II, who was unable to put this instrument to any profitable use. France had suffered a certain loss of prestige through her defeats in the Seven Years' War, but even at the height of

its glory the Prussian army had some hidden defects. Its institutions and equipment needed modification, and it was not long before the high command and officer corps were reorganized. Reform became essential.

The infantry regiments, cavalry and artillery kept their previous numbers and make-up, but the American War of Independence had demonstrated the importance of light infantry. The first reforms of Frederick William II, begun in 1787, involved the creation of one regiment of foot *Jäger* and three of light infantry. In 1788, the same time as the infantry were being reformed, there was a curious innovation, the formation of the Bosniak regiment, lancers dressed and equipped in the Turkish style and attached to the hussar units. A horse-drawn artillery corps was also introduced.

It was this reorganized army, under

Marshal Charles William Ferdinand, Duke of Brunswick, which confronted the new French Revolutionary army. The famous 'cannonade' of Valmy in 1792 revealed to the world the failure of an old-fashioned and obsolescent command system. The campaign ended in 1795 after a pitiful retreat by the Prussian army, hampered by bad weather.

The king and the General Staff retained some features of the army's uniforms, weapons and equipment, while making several reforms. For instance, the year 1788 saw the replacement of the typical infantry tricorne by the *Kaskett*, a hat with two flaps edged with white braid turned up in front and behind, which could be lowered in bad weather. The grenadiers wore a grenade on the front, and the musketeers and fusiliers the King's cypher or the Prussian eagle. The cap was surmounted by a small plume. Infantry officers like the cuirassiers and dragoons, retained the tricorne, now more elongated in the fashion of the time.

The cutaway coat became closer-fitting, with lapels and regimental buttonhole loops. Regiment No. 6, the Grenadier Guard Battalion, was allowed to keep its traditional grenadier mitre cap, and the infantry and artillery continued to wear blue, except for the light infantry and *Jäger* who wore green, a colour much beloved by riflemen.

The traditions of the Prussian army demanded a spotless turn-out, enforced by iron discipline and unremitting drill. Yet impeccable as it was in peacetime, the army finished the French campaign of 1792 in terrible weather conditions, decimated by dysentery, with no greatcoats and no rain protection, its appearance and morale in tatters.

It was undoubtedly this experience which brought about the introduction of long grey or unbleached canvas overalls intended to protect the garments beneath, in spite of the gaiters already worn below the knee. The hair-style was simplified and the queue, tied with black ribbon, appreciably shortened. Once again it was on the battlefield that the true 'battledress' of the armies of the time evolved, although the common infantry-man still went to war without a greatcoat. The cavalry were more fortunate; after 1790 all units were equipped with a voluminous coat or cloak of thick cloth with a high collar of regimental colour. The *garde du corps*, gendarmes and cuirassiers abandoned their iron breastplates, and the tails of their *Kollers* were shortened.

The dragoons still dressed in pale blue, and wore the same cut of uniform as the infantry of the line. There was relatively little change in the colourful turn-out of the hussars, with their dolmans and pelisses lavishly decorated with braid and cording in the facing colour. Coats could now be worn buttoned up. For campaign wear all hussar regiments were issued with long grey button-through overalls protecting their white cloth or leather full-dress breeches. The head-dress was still the *mirliton* or, particularly for officers, the big fur *kolpak* with gold or silver cords and flounders.

Both foot and mounted musicians were distinguished mainly by regimentals in the reversed colours of their units. The infantry also wore heavy braiding on the sleeves.

Like the infantry, the artillery adopted a dark blue coat of the new cut with black lapels, cuffs and collar, while the pioneers and sappers kept their orange facings. In 1797 the new fusilier battalions were issued with dark green coats and black leather accoutrements, thus getting rid of all conspicuous colours.

The accession in 1798 of the young King Frederick William III, who was even more conservative than his father, did little to alter the army's organization, style and uniform. In 1800 the Bosniak regiment of lancers was converted into *Towarczys*, with a blue and red uniform *à la polonaise*. Some of the changes of dress and equipment ordered by the new king were actually regressive, especially for the infantry. His pettifogging mind was interested only in the details of clothing. The cloth and materials used were of poor quality, uniforms were cut more skimpily in a misplaced attempt to economize. The lapels and turnbacks ceased to be functional and became mere strips of cloth sewn onto the coat. The collar was raised even higher, right under the chin. Waistcoats were dispensed with, leaving only a tiny remnant sewn inside the bottom of the coat.

As early as 1798 a number of facing colours were changed, and the tricorne was restored to the rank and file of the infantry, pioneer-sappers and artillery. By order of the king the grenadiers found themselves issued with a new type of head-dress with the headband in the facing colour. The peaked front, in leather edged with a band of black wool, bore the Prussian eagle, and the whole was decorated with a white plume.

But in 1801 there appeared, as an experiment, the cylindrical shako with leather peak, first used by the foot *Jäger*, who wore short black gaiters or leather boots. For the cuirassiers and dragoons the hats, which were now bicornes, plumes and collar height continued to grow. They wore a waistcoat beneath their *Koller*. Most of the dragoon regiments kept their traditional appearance and facing colours.

In 1802 the infantry and cavalry (cuirassiers and dragoons) received straight lapels in place of the previously scalloped ones. Only officers kept the long-tailed coat. As for the hussars, after 1796 they gave up the big fur *kolpak* for the *mirliton*, except for the old No. 2 (Ziethen) Regiment. The

artillery, the cut of whose coat was the same as the infantry's, but blue with black facings, wore the tricorne and overalls at exercise and on campaign.

There could be no better record of the actual appearance and style of an army still thoroughly under the influence and tradition of Frederick the Great than the admirable collections of fine coloured prints published between 1789 and 1803 by the contemporary Berlin artists Ch. Cr. Horvath, G. Thieme and A. L. Ramm.

At the time of their engagement in the coalition wars the Prussian troops stood out by virtue of their impeccable dress and discipline and the strictness of their training and behaviour, in stark contrast with the free-and-easy manner and sloppy dress of their opponents, the redoubtable *sansculottes*. But it would have taken more than the spirit and tradition of Frederick the Great to prevent the disastrous defeats which overtook the Prussian army in 1806.

Early in 1792 Francis II succeeded Leopold II as Emperor of Austria, Prussia's ally. France had already declared war in reply to the allies' manifesto by invading Belgium, which belonged to the Empire. The army of Austria-Hungary was a patchwork of nationalities and languages spread over a number of the countries of central Europe, factors which did not assist either the recruitment or maintenance of a large army. But a hundred years of organization and tradition had endowed it with a relatively stable structure, which was to prove its worth, in spite of the setbacks of the Seven Years' War, during the reign of Empress Maria Theresa and her sons and successors Joseph II (1765–90) and Leopold II (1790–2).

It was mainly the ordinances and regulations of 1767, 1790 and 1800 which gave the Austrian army its characteristic appearance and fighting ability during the great

The legendary 'white coats'
of the Austrian cavalry,
Dragoon regiment, *c*. 1793.

conflicts it faced between 1792 and 1803. This army, so varied both in its origins and recruitment, the legendary 'white coats', were to bear the brunt of the French onslaught and put up a loyal resistance under standards of the double-headed eagle. On the Rhine, in Alsace and in the 'lines of Wissenburg', old Marshal Dagobert Wurmser, preceded by his Pandours and Croats, the fearsome 'red cloaks', was able to gain his first campaign successes.

After its defeat at Jemappes the Austrian army had to evacuate Belgium, but in 1793 the Prince of Coburg managed to repulse the French. This was also the first feather in the cap of the young Archduke Charles, the Emperor's brother and tough future adversary of Napoleon Bonaparte. The entire weight of the struggle fell upon the Austrian army, left alone after the retreat of the Prussians, who were obliged to fall back along the line from the Rhine to the Alps. It was an effort which it could only sustain with the support of the French *émigrés*, the army of Condé and the Princes.

But after 1796 a new phase in the war was to bring the French army up against Archduke Charles, the victor of Würzburg, while Bonaparte forced Marshal Wurmser to surrender at Mantua with the honours of war, 'standards and flags flying', and pushed on as far as Semmering the following year.

The second coalition war broke out in 1799 and the two nations continued to clash on the battlefields of southern Germany at Stockach and at Novi. It was at this point that Russia went to the assistance of the Archduke Charles, with Suvarov's fresh troops crossing the St Gotthard and defeating the French at the 'Devil's Bridge' near Andermatt. The famous battle painter Albrecht Adam gives an eye-witness account of the style and appearance of the rival armies in the same period, in 1797:

I was roused to enthusiasm by the smart and colourful uniforms of the French Revolutionary army, the keen spirit, the very soul, the characteristically wild faces of those soldiers, and their strange way of moving. The most striking contrast was produced by the *Austrian armies*. We saw them pass by, calm and grave, mostly in serried columns, correctly dressed even in mid-campaign. Resigned to hardship, never forgetting their discipline, they always made an impression to be respected. But the character of nationalities as diverse as those composing the Austrian army was bound to be of keen interest to me, and nothing attracted me more strongly than an Austrian camp. I sketched everything I could see, and cherished the idea that some day I might become a military painter.

The Austrian infantry consisted of 'German' and 'Hungarian' regiments, both wearing the traditional white coat with facings of various colours, but the Germans having white breeches with black gaiters and the Hungarians close-fitting pale blue ankle-length pantaloons. The coat had no lapels and buttoned up the front. For the centre companies, the tricorne gave way to a cap made of boiled leather, the *Kaskett* with the F II cypher in front. The grenadiers wore fur caps with a yellow and black cockade. The officers wore the tricorne.

In 1798 a new kind of head-dress was introduced for the infantry and the cavalry, with the exception of the hussars. It was a black leather helmet in use in Bavaria since 1790. The volunteer *Jäger* corps of the period were distinguished by their iron-grey coats with green facings, like the famous *Kaiserjäger*. The artillery wore brown with scarlet collar and cuffs. White coats with red facings and breeches and gold embroidery became standard wear for the officers of the General Staff. For the whole army, the hair was worn in a *queue*.

Cavalry uniforms were still distinguished by a great variety of colours and an

OVERPAGE The engagement on the Teufelsbrücke (Devil's Bridge) in 1799, by Johann Baptist Seele. The picture shows an episode from the wars between the Russians and the French in the St Gotthard Pass. The Russian grenadiers (*left*) are wearing the pointed steel helmets whose design was appropriated from the Prussian army in the eighteenth century.

Austrian hussars and Uhlans. The hussars, originally Hungarian by nationality, were fine swordsmen, and their uniforms derived from the Hungarian national costume. The Uhlans, or lancers, came into being in 1784, and originated from Poland. Engraving by J. B. Seele.

individual style dear to the soldiers of that army. As early as 1767 the cuirassiers were equipped with the white *Kollet* buttoning up the front and faced with the most variegated colours, worn under the black cuirass of which only the front plate was retained. The yellow and black-plumed tricorne gave way to a crested helmet around 1799.

The same head-dress was also adopted by the dragoons and *chevau-légers* who had previously worn the *Kaskett*. The former were given white uniforms with different coloured facings and the plumed tricorne, the latter wore either white or green and the *Kaskett*. Curiously enough, from 1798 to 1801 all the dragoon regiments were converted into 'light dragoons' with crested helmets, green jackets, white breeches and boots.

The hussars, originally Hungarian by nationality, fine and tireless swordsmen, were celebrated for their proud bearing and their horsemanship. As for their equipment and uniform, they managed to keep up the old Magyar traditions in the service of their king and emperor. They could be found on every field of battle. Their uniform derived from the Hungarian national costume and consisted first and foremost of the colourful waist-length dolman, lavishly adorned with black and yellow braiding, and the fur-trimmed pelisse. The legs were clad in tight multi-coloured pantaloons ornamented with frogging, and the boots were of the Hungarian pattern, often in coloured leather. On campaign, carrying their weapons, bulky baggage and forage bags, wearing the *mirliton*, and preceded by trumpeters oddly dressed in the German style and wearing the tricorne, the Hungarian hussars also adopted buttoned overalls.

Classed as light cavalry, the lancers, the Uhlans, were introduced in 1784. Orig-

inally they wore a sky-blue *kurtka* with yellow collar, lapels and cuffs, and for headdress a Polish-style *chapska* trimmed with fur. The uniform was white in 1786, but in 1792 it was changed to green with red facings, worn with a plumed yellow *chapska*. The lancers came from Poland, were imitated by Austria and by Prussia, and were later introduced in France.

To protect its frontiers, the Austro-Hungarian Empire had recourse to a network of garrison units, the *Grenzer*, equipped as light troops. The soldiers were often married, and were recruited from among the native populations of the administrative districts or 'Generalats'. They partly retained their national dress, but were being more rationally equipped as early as 1767. The infantry had grey jackets, Hungarian-style pantaloons worn with laced boots, a peakless shako in plain felt and red cloaks.

Since the seventeenth century the Habsburg-Lorraine dynasty had had palace guards of its own, both foot and horse. Foremost among these were the Watchguard (*Arcieren-Leibgarde*), and after them the Trabant Guard (*Trabanten-Leibgarde*), wearing red with black facings and gold braid, and carrying sword and halberd. They were equipped with the crested helmet in 1800. A company of *Leibgardeinfantrie* was on special attachment to the Hofburg and dressed in grey, with white breeches and tricorne.

The noble Hungarian horse guard, created in 1760, wore an opulent red uniform with lavish silver braiding, panther skins and plumed *kolpaks*. In 1782 the Polish Guard in turn was dressed in a white *confederatka*, red and blue coats with lavish gold trimmings, and red leather boots. A lancer unit, it was abolished in 1791. But none of these units ever saw active service.

There was, however, another force, the army of the French *émigrés*, whose loyalist spirit, fidelity and fighting qualities were to be of the greatest assistance to the Austrians and the states of southern Germany after the death of Louis XVI and into the 1800s. The first groups of *émigré* soldiers were assembled in 1791, but the movement took on greater proportions in 1792 with the exodus from France not only of many senior officers and subalterns but also of whole units, which left the country to fight in a dismal fratricidal conflict against the 'patriots' who had become their bitterest enemies. These units were first reorganized on the right bank of the Rhine, in Coblenz and Rastatt, mainly by Joseph-Louis of Bourbon, Prince of Condé, on and after 1793. Although scattered across Switzerland, the Netherlands, England and Russia, they went on fighting until around 1803.

Apart from the infantry and cavalry which were largely drawn from the aristocracy, élite units consisting mainly of *émigré* officers belonging to the Condé army were either equipped with French-style uniforms, or retained their previous dress and equipment as members of the old royal army. Thus the hussar regiments of Berchény and Saxe, partly made up of *émigrés*, kept their old dolmans and pelisses. A typical case is that of the Royal Allemand Cavalry Regiment, which left France, bag and baggage, led by its colonel, to enter the service of Austria. It kept its blue uniform with crimson facings and its lavish white braid; only the white plumes in its fur caps were changed to the yellow and black of the Austrian army.

Numerous infantry and cavalry formations were taken into the pay of the various states allied against France. The mere mention of units such as the Enghien Dragoons, the Rohan Infantry, the Bussy Chasseurs, the Mirabeau Legion, the

FRANCE

Light Infantry, 1800   General, 1796   Grenadier of the Swiss Guards Regiment, 1792   Infantry Officer. 1800   Infantryman, 1795

FRANCE

Officer of the Consular Guard, 1800   Cuirassier of the King's Cuirassier Regiment   Horse Artillery, 1800   Hussar of the 3rd Hussar Regiment, 1797   Officer of the 6th Mounted Chasseurs, 1792–1800

Helvetian Republic, Hussar, 1798–1800

Cisalpine Republic, NCO of the Lombard Cisalpine Legion, 1797

Batavian Republic, 2nd Cavalry Regiment, 1801

France, Artilleryman of the Polish Danube Legion, 1800

Batavian Republic, Chasseur, 1801

Russia, Officer of the Horse Artillery, 1797–1801

Russia, Chasseur of the 14th Chasseur Battalion, 1797

Spain, Grenadier of the Zamora Infantry Regiment

Württemberg, Infantryman, 1804

Baden, Officer of the Hussars in parade uniform, 1793

ABOVE The Austrian
infantry around 1800
consisted of 'German' and
'Hungarian' regiments both
wearing the traditional
white coat. Engraving by
J. B. Seele.

RIGHT The Austrian artillery
of 1800 wore brown and
scarlet collar and cuffs.
Engraving by J. B. Seele.

Portugal, Infantry officer, 1800

Bavaria, Trooper of the 2nd Regiment of Light Horse, 1790–1800

Sardinia, Officer of the Light Infantry, 1792

Hessen-Darmstadt, Trooper of the Light Horse Regiment, 1799

England, Infantryman of the Antichamp Infantry Regiment (French emigré troops), 1795

ENGLAND
Grenadier of the 1st Regiment of Foot Guards, 1800

Artilleryman of the Horse Artillery, 1800

Officer of the 1st Regiment of Foot Guards, 1790

Musketeer of the 14th Regiment of Foot (Bedfordshire Regiment), 1794

Officer of the 15th Light Dragoon Regiment, 1793

AUSTRIA

Dragoon of the 14th Light
Dragoon Regiment
(Leveehr's), 1798–1801

Officer of the Light
Infantry, 1798–1801

Hussar of Wurmser's
Hussar Regiment,
1798–1800

Grenadier of the 1st
Infantry Regiment, 1799

Officer of Wurmser's
Freicorps, 1798

PRUSSIA, Coalition Wars

Hussar of von Werner's
Hussar Regiment, 1792

48th Infantry Regiment,
1792

Fusilier Officer of von
Ernest's Fusilier Battalion,
No. 19, 1800

Officer of the Bosniaks in
summer uniform, 1792

Musketeer, Infantry
Regiment, 1792

Baschy Hussars, the Damas Legion and the British Uhlans will indicate the wide variety of colours to be found in the uniforms of these soldiers, who were sometimes reduced to fighting in a wretched, shabby 'battledress'. To distinguish these royalists from the other allied troops they wore white cockades and white armbands stamped with a black *fleur-de-lys* (a sign of mourning) on the left arm.

Elsewhere certain states of Rhineland Germany, threatened by the French invasion, rallied to the Austro-Hungarian flag and took part in the campaigns of the Coalitions.

Of the score or more principalities constituting the Germany of the late eighteenth century the margraviate of Baden was one of the first to be drawn into military involvement by the advance of the French armies beyond the Rhine. The clothing and equipment of the Baden troops were derived from the Prussian model, the infantry regiments wearing blue with red and yellow facings and Prussian-style grenadier and fusilier mitre caps. The *garde du corps* originally wore yellow with a tricorn hat, but changed its uniform to white in 1799 and again to sky-blue trimmed with red in 1801. The dragoon company wore blue with black facings. The hussars wore the green dolmans and pelisses with yellow lace and red collars and cuffs. The artillery wore black. In 1803 the uniform became closer-fitting and the lapels straight.

Like Baden, the duchy of Württemberg clung closely to the Prussian example. It had a larger army than Baden, with a more effective fighting structure, developed during its alliance with Austria in the Seven Years' War.

The creation in 1786 of the infantry regiment known as the *Kapregiment*, intended for duty in the East Indies, gave rise to a new type of uniform which broke with tradition. The dark blue uniform with yellow collar, cuffs and lapels and white breeches was accompanied by a new type of crested black leather helmet with plume, introduced to the entire army in 1799. This unit was equipped wholly at the expense of Duke Charles Eugène.

In 1789 all regiments wore this dress with variously coloured facings, except for the grenadier battalion (the future guard regiment), which wore a fur cap. Then in 1799 Duke Frederick formed a company known as the 'black chasseurs', with a dark green uniform and bicorn hat. The cavalry consisted of one regiment of *Kreis-Dragoner*, in blue with red and yellow facings and bicornes with black plumes. In 1792 this was changed to a blue coat with black collar, lapels and cuffs and red turnbacks, worn with a crested black helmet. In 1795 a further modification changed lapels and collar to red.

At the same time a new unit was created and divided into three squadrons, the *garde du corps*, the *Leibjäger*, and the *chevau-légers*, each distinguished by the details and colours of its uniform. The hussar regiment in green with yellow lace, black collar and cuffs and red breeches was disbanded in 1798. The artillery wore pale blue with black, the facing colour of nearly all the artillery corps of the time.

The character and appearance of the Bavarian army was comparable to that of the Austrian army. With the merging of the army of the Palatinate (*Kurpfalz*) with that of Bavaria in 1777, a period when pale blue was still predominant, there was a sharp increase in the number of units. The first alteration in dress came in 1785 with the introduction of white uniforms for the infantry, a characteristic colour which was extended to the entire Bavarian army in 1789.

At the same time the American-born

minister Benjamin Rumford introduced a metal helmet, with a white crest for the grenadiers and black for fusiliers. The blue uniform was made tight-fitting, with different coloured facings, grey trousers and short black gaiters *à la hongroise*. The cuirassiers and dragoons wore the same white uniform, but the light horse created by Rumford in 1790 wore iron-grey with coloured collar, lapels and cuffs. The year 1800 saw the introduction of the big leather helmet with black crest for the whole army and the very distinctive pale blue uniforms which the Bavarian army subsequently retained. After 1791 the artillery uniform was dark blue with black lapels, the collar and cuffs piped with red. The ancient palace guard, the *Hartschiere*, wore the court livery, blue and black trimmed with silver, and a red cloak. It was armed with a *couse* (halberd).

The other sovereign German states of the day tended to model their arms, equipment, and especially their uniforms, on the example of contemporary Prussia. The most important of these include the landgraviates of Hesse-Darmstadt and Hessen-Kassel and the duchies of Brunswick, Anhalt and Oldenburg. Around 1803 Nassau followed the Bavarian model.

The electorate of Saxony was by tradition a loyal ally of Austria-Hungary, and since the great reorganization of 1765 the infantry had worn white coats with variously coloured collars, lapels and cuffs, tight-fitting Hungarian-style pantaloons in the facing colour, trimmed with Hungarian knots, and tricornes, except for the grenadiers, who wore fur caps. The cut of the uniform was changed in 1771 and again in about 1800. Only the *Leibgrenadier-Garde* continued to wear the fur cap, pale yellow facings, white breeches and waistcoat, and black or white gaiters, according to the season – their uniform since 1764.

Of the cavalry, the *garde du corps*, carabiniers and cuirassiers adopted the pale yellow *Koller*, the latter with black cuirasses. The dragoons, like the light horse, kept the traditional red coat and tricorne which they were still wearing after 1803. In 1791 the hussar regiment was alone in adopting white dolmans with sky blue facings and braiding, sky-blue pelisses trimmed with blue braid, and black *mirlitons*. The artillery retained the dark green first introduced in 1730.

Since 1714 the electorate of Hanover had found itself in a peculiar situation through its union with the throne of Great Britain under George I. During the reign of George III Britain became the determining influence on the Hanoverian army and its institutions.

The British army was among the bitterest adversaries of the French. Its 'Redcoats' had become famous both for their organization and their strict discipline. Their uniforms underwent numerous changes. The Household Cavalry – the Life Guards, in red with blue facings, and the Royal Horse Guards, traditionally dressed in blue, together with the footguards, and the line regiments, were clothed in accordance with the Royal Warrants of 1768 and 1796. The normal head-dress was tricornes with fur caps for the grenadiers. The Royal Horse Artillery wore 'Tarleton' helmets and dark blue hussar jackets with red facings from the time of their introduction in 1793. But the influence of changing fashion and various improvements made themselves felt, particularly between 1796 and 1800. Iron discipline meant the strict observation of clothing regulations by the rank and file, although officers could give rein to their fancy by blending elements of civilian dress with the prescribed uniform.

In the cavalry, hats, red coats, white breeches and boots were the normal wear,

The 'Russisch Kaiserliche Cavallerie' or Russian cavalry
around 1800. Engraving from life by L. Ebner.

The 'Russisch Kaiserliche Infanterie' or Russian infantry of
line and light infantry around 1800.

but after 1784 the light dragoons were distinguished by their blue jackets and crested 'Tarleton' helmets. After 1796 cut-away coats and jackets for both infantry and cavalry were superseded by closed patterns.

The numerous volunteer and militia units raised after 1799 were distinguished by their crested 'Tarleton' helmets, but their uniforms varied considerably in design and colour from unit to unit. The introduction of the 'stovepipe' shako dates from 1800.

Scottish units were still distinguished by their own Highland dress with plaid, short jacket, and the characteristic hummel bonnet. All through the British army, both in the infantry and the cavalry, musicians wore the most fanciful uniforms, which they retained even under fire on the battlefield.

While Nordic countries such as Denmark and Sweden had their own national style of uniform, it is interesting to note that between 1790 and 1803 Russia displayed some curious developments, while retaining the traditional green uniforms. But it was to Catherine II's edict of 1786 that the Russian army owed the introduction of a standard uniform, almost modern in its design and appearance, overturning all the received ideas of the time. It was ordered for all units except hussars and the *garde du corps*.

The coat, with straight lapels and shortened tails turned back at thigh level in the facing colour, was worn with red trousers reinforced below the knee with buttoned leather false boots. The head-dress was in the shape of a black leather helmet with a coloured wool crest passing from one temple to the other. Ten years later Paul I abolished this practical garb and returned to the strict Prussian model. In 1803 his son Alexander I introduced the shako for the infantry regiments, the officers retaining their cocked hats and gold aiguillettes.

In the convulsions of the campaigns of 1792–1803, France had succeeded in setting up the Batavian Republic in Holland, the Cisalpine Republic in Italy, and the Helvetic Republic in Switzerland. When the authorities created and levied new units in these occupied countries they had them equipped and uniformed according to the French pattern.

The Napoleonic Wars
1800-15

4

ECKART KLESSMANN

In Thevenin's painting of the
Battle of Jena, executed in
1810 for Berthier,
Napoleon's Chief-of-Staff
rides immediately behind
the Emperor.

The uniforms worn during the first fifteen years of the nineteenth century represent the most elaborate display of pomp in the whole history of military dress. These fifteen years virtually moulded the appearance of armies throughout the entire century. Contemporary observers regarded the extravagant uniforms of Napoleon's army with unreserved astonishment. When the people of Berlin first came face to face with the enemy troops as they marched into the city after their victories at Jena and Auerstädt in 1806, they openly marvelled at the sappers with their axes, leather aprons, busbies and gigantic beards (a prototype which the majority of states copied from France and which persisted well into the nineteenth century), at the gold-bedecked drum-majors of towering athletic build (who were also prototypical), at the iron-clad cuirassiers with black horsehair plumes on their helmets (as worn to this day by the republican guards of France and Italy), and finally at Napoleon's élite troops, the *Garde Impériale*. A Berlin observer could 'scarcely take his eyes off the rich, brightly-coloured uniforms' of the latter 'in which the full power of the French national colours, thousand-fold echoes of red, blue and white, riveted the eye'. Another Berliner testified that some citizens even tried to join these élite troops, 'The allure of the Guards' fine uniforms was the principal attraction.'

The uniforms of the European armies underwent a fundamental change in the early years of the nineteenth century. The leather or felt shako became the principal head-dress, replacing the felt bicorne hitherto in use, although it continued to be worn by officers, including generals, and in these ranks it predominated. The cavalry began to be distinguished by crested helmets, plumed metal helmets, and the Polish

chapska – these also made isolated appearances in the infantry, as the flugel cap (*mirliton*), previously typical of the hussars, disappeared. The low fur cap of the hussars also became less common, although in France it became the distinguishing mark of the élite cavalry troops, and the tall fur caps widely worn by grenadiers of the line infantry came over the years to be the exclusive mark of the guards.

The basic colours of the nations had already been firmly established in the eighteenth century; blue as the colour of Prussia, red as the colour of Great Britain. The Russians appeared dressed in dark green, the Austrians in white and the French were in either white or blue. It was only after the French Revolution, when the tricolour was adopted as the national flag, that the blue–white–red combination became the basis for French infantry uniform.

As the size of national armies increased standardization was more widely introduced, despite a vast number of exceptions. Evidence of this trend towards standardization is shown by the fact that after 1807 the various line infantry regiments were less commonly distinguished by different coloured markings (facings, collars and cuffs), but instead by regimental numbers on buttons and head-dress. Moreover, the troops of the Confederation of the Rhine, allied to France, were given a uniform of French cut, although the colour worn by the infantry was normally white. This trend was emphasized in 1810 when Napoleon ordered standard uniforms for both infantry and cavalry musicians, with the exception of the Guards. Musicians had previously worn either a mixture of colours (with the distinctive colour of the regiment predominating), or they had been dressed entirely according to the personal taste of the regimental commander. Loose linen

OPPOSITE The young people of Leipzig lead the newly arrived French to their billets. On 18 October 1806 – four days after the battles of Jena and Auerstädt – the army corps of Major Davout occupied Leipzig. The French infantry are still wearing hats, for the infantry shako had only just been introduced. In the centre of the picture is a carabinier of the Light Infantry with a tall fur cap, and on the far left a fusilier of the 57th Line Regiment. Painting by Christian Gottfried Heinrich Geissler (1770–1844).

FRANCE 1800–15

Musician of the 3rd (Dutch) Regiment of the Imperial Guard

Grenadier of the 3rd (Dutch) Regiment of the Imperial Guard

Drum Major of the 1st Regiment of the Imperial Guard

Grenadier of the 1st Regiment of the Imperial Guard

Grenadier of the 1st Regiment of the Imperial Guard (in cloak)

FRANCE 1800–15

Marine Guard

Engineer of the Imperial Guard

Sapper of the Imperial Guard Chasseurs

Foot Artillery of the Imperial Guard, artisan

Chasseur of the Imperial Guard (in greatcoat)

FRANCE 1800-15
Grenadier of the Mounted
Grenadier Guards

Mounted Chasseur
Regiment of the Imperial
Guard

Lancer of the 2nd (Dutch)
Regiment of the Imperial
Guard

Dragoon Guard
(Empress's Dragoons)

Lancer of the 2nd (Dutch)
Regiment of the Imperial
Guard (Field-Marshal
Mässig's)

FRANCE
Adjutant to Marshal
Berthier, 1809

Élite gendarme of the
Imperial Guard in full
dress, 1813

Guard of Honour, 1813,
2nd Regiment

Gendarme orderly, 1806

Mameluke, 1808, attached
to the Guards Chasseur
Regiment

'The Battle of Marengo' by
Louis-François Lejeune
(1775–1848). Lejeune took
part in this battle, on 14
June 1800, as a captain of
sappers on the staff of
General Berthier. He has
depicted himself on the far
right, with a white armband,
on horseback among the
Austrian prisoners.

FRANCE
Grenadier, 1812 (5th
Regiment of Infantry)

Fusilier, 1808

Grenadier, 1806

Grenadier in cloak, 1813

Officer of a grenadier
company, 1806

FRANCE
Bandmaster of the 67th
Infantry Regiment, 1809

Light Infantryman, 1806

Light Infantryman, 1808

Bandmaster of the 9th
Infantry Regiment, 1809

Chasseur Officer, 1813

Light Infantryman of
Isenburg's Regiment of
Infantry, 1808

Light Infantryman of the
Prince of Neuchatel's
Battalion (Berthier), 1810

Light Infantryman of the
Portuguese Legion, 1812

Grenadier of the 'Prussia'
Regiment, 1806

Grenadier of La Tour
d'Auvergne's Regiment,
1808

FRANCE
Surgeon, 1812

Driver of an artillery train,
1813

Lieutenant of Foot
Artillery, 1811

Gunner of Mounted
Artillery, 1812

Pioneer, 1809

ABOVE 'The Battle of Friedland, 14 June 1807' by Horace Vernet (1789–1863). Napoleon is seen here amongst his troops.

OPPOSITE 'Louis-François Lejeune' by Paulin Guérin (1783–1855). The portrait shows the painter and colonel Lejeune in the uniform which he designed in 1808.

trousers (*pantaloons*) also became standard for infantry, and linen overalls with leather strapping on the inside leg for cavalry (both for active service) and waterproof oilskin covers for the shakos.

Naturally there were constant exceptions, and these were often more marked than the concern for standardization. Thus in many states the hussars kept to the old practice of clothing each regiment differently, and four of the thirty-one mounted regiments of French chasseurs wore a uniform cut in the style of the hussars, although in reality a long-skirted coat was prescribed – in dark green as was customary for chasseurs, who were partly recruited from foresters. It also remained common practice for soldiers to be equipped with three uniforms: dress uniform (*grande tenue*), active service uniform (*petite tenue* or *tenue de route*) and barracks uniform (*tenue de quartier*), each as different as possible from the others.

As already mentioned, a special cult was made in France of the uniforms of musicians. The appearance of the military bands, which always marched at the head of the troops, was until 1810 the concern of

FRANCE, 1800–15
Cuirassier   Dragoon   Carabinier, 1810   Mounted Chasseur of the   Carabinier, 1805
                                                                          26th Regiment

FRANCE, 1800–15
Lancer of the 7th (Polish)   Lancer of the 1st (French)   Belgian Prince Arenberg's   Chasseur of the 13th   Dragoon of the 7th
Regiment of Lancers   Regiment of Lancers   Light Horse, 1807 (27th   Regiment of Mounted   Dragoon Regiment, 1810,
                                          Regiment of Mounted   Chasseurs, élite   élite
                                          Chasseurs)

FRANCE

Trumpeter of the Mounted
Chasseurs, 1810

Trumpeter of the
Carabiniers, 1809–10

Trumpeter of the 12th
Cuirassier Regiment

Trumpeter of the 17th
Dragoons (new uniform,
1812)

Trumpeter of the 1st
Hussars, 1807–8

FRANCE

Hussar of the 3rd Hussar
Regiment, 1810

Hussar of the 5th Hussar
Regiment, 1808

Hussar of the 7th Hussar
Regiment, 1808

Hussar of the 1st Hussar
Regiment, 1808

Hussar of the 8th Hussar
Regiment, 1809

the officer commanding the regiment at the time; and their appearance could never be sumptuous or colourful enough to satisfy him. Thus the drum-majors, who marched in front of the band – the ones celebrated by Heinrich Heine – wore either fur caps, crowned with coloured pompoms and a colossal plume, or bicornes. These last were also worn by the *chefs de musique*. The musicians themselves were normally only supplied with a shako, but those of the 9th Line Infantry Regiment and the 17th Light Infantry Regiment also wore *chapskas*, which were usually only worn by the lancers.

In 1810, when Napoleon ordered a completely standard uniform for bandsmen – green with yellow trimmings – he met with no support. Between 1812 and 1815 only a few regimental bands were dressed in accordance with this order. Most continued as before. Besides, in many cases the old uniforms had to be used until worn out, for new ones were not available from the stores.

Napoleon's marshals, Bernadotte, Berthier and Mortier, liked to dress their staffs in elaborate uniforms. Bernadotte, acutely jealous of Napoleon, copied the uniforms of Napoleon's chasseurs, but altered the colours in order to contrast them with those of his rival. General Chief of Staff Berthier, however, went one important step further: he commissioned Louis-François Lejeune, a colonel on his staff and a talented painter, to design a special uniform.

In his memoirs, Lejeune gives this account:

The prince [Berthier] had commissioned me to design a special uniform for our troops. I chose one in the Hungarian style: a coat of black cloth, a white dolman with gold braiding, breeches and shako of scarlet cloth, the latter surmounted by a tuft of heron's feathers. These various garments embellished in the richest fash-

ion with gold braid, facings and buttons. A rich sash made of black silk with gold barrells, a small cartridge pouch, a sabretache and a sabre with a Damascus blade completed the outfit. Our parade horses were of Arab blood, pale greys with flowing, well-groomed manes and tails, bridled after the manner of the hussars. A panther skin with scalloped red and gold edging covered the saddle.

When Napoleon made his triumphal entry into Madrid on 8 December 1808, the troops of his general chief of staff wore the uniforms designed by Lejeune for the first time.

Joachim Murat occupied a special position in all this. Marshal of France, Grand Duke of Berg, King of Naples, and in addition supreme head of the French cavalry, he always appeared on the battlefield dressed like a brightly-coloured parrot. Napoleon, his brother-in-law, liked to refer to him as 'King Franconi', after the manager of the largest circus in France. Murat wore a different uniform almost every day, invariably choosing skin-tight breeches, with boots of supple morocco leather in yellow, red or green, his battledress embroidered with gold, his fur cap set with jewel-encrusted brooches, when he was not wearing a brightly-coloured *chapska* or – on very rare occasions – the prescribed head-dress of a marshal. The Neapolitan Hussar Guards who had formed his escort since 1808 appeared in richly braided yellow uniforms, and were always mounted on dun horses with white manes and tails.

In the face of such a cult of individuality, the French hussars of the line did not want to be made to feel inferior. Not only did each regiment dressed in a completely different uniform, but they were also remarkable for their splendidly coloured plumes. Napoleon's decree of 9 November 1810 had indeed strictly forbidden these plumes on hussars' shakos and fur caps, but the

PRUSSIA

Fusilier of the 5th Fusilier
Battalion (von Wedel's)

NCO of von Rheinbaden's
Grenadier Battalion

Officer of the 5th Fusilier
Battalion (von Wedel's)

Musketeer of the 23rd
Regiment of Infantry (von
Winning's)

Grenadier of the 23rd
Regiment of Infantry (von
Winning's)

PRUSSIA

Gunner of the Foot
Artillery

Gunner of the Field
Artillery

Officer of the
Sharpshooters' Regiment

Officer of the 55th
Regiment of Infantry (von
Manstein's)

Grenadier of von Losthin's
Grenadier Battalion

PRUSSIA

Hussar of the 10th
Regiment of Hussars (von
Usedom's)

Hussar of the 2nd
Regiment of Hussars (von
Rudorff's)

Towarczy of the Towarczy
Regiment

Hussar of the 5th
Regiment of Hussars (von
Prittwitz's)

Hussar of the 6th
Regiment of Hussars (von
Pletz's)

PRUSSIA

Dragoon of the 10th
Regiment of Dragoons (von
Manstein's)

Cuirassier of the 11th
Regiment of Cuirassiers
(Gens d'Armes)

Trumpeter of the 12th
Regiment of Cuirassiers
(von Bünting's)
(walking-out uniform)

Officer of the 13th
Regiment of Dragoons
(von Rouquette's)

Cuirassier of the 2nd
Regiment of Cuirassiers
(von Beeren's)

PRUSSIA, 1808–15
Grenadier of the Guards
Infantry Regiment on
parade

Grenadier of the Guards
Infantry Regiment
(Field-Marshal Mässig's)

Chasseur of the Guards
Chasseur Battalion

Fusilier of the Guards
Fusilier Battalion
(Field-Marshal Mässig's)

Gunner of the Guards
Mounted Artillery

PRUSSIA, 1808–15
Musketeer of the 1st
West Prussian Infantry
Regiment

Sharpshooter of the
Silesian Sharpshooters
Battalion

Chasseur volunteer of von
Reiche's Foreign Chasseur
Battalion

Soldier of the Silesian
Territorial Reserve

Infantryman of the
4th Reserve Infantry
Regiment

PRUSSIA, 1808–15

Cuirassier of the Garde du Corps Regiment, 1813

Cossack of the Guards Cossack Volunteer Squadron, 1813

Chasseur of the Guards Chasseur Volunteer Squadron, 1813

Uhlan of the *Leibuhlanen* Squadron, 1812

Dragoon of the Normal Dragoon Squadron, 1812

PRUSSIA 1808–15

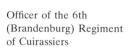

Chasseur of Lützow's Freikorps

Officer of the 6th (Brandenburg) Regiment of Cuirassiers

Uhlan of the Brandenburg Uhlan Regiment

Dragoon of the Lithuanian Dragoon Regiment

Hussar of the 2nd Silesian Regiment of Hussars

GREAT BRITAIN

Sapper of the 2nd Regiment of Foot Guards (Coldstream), 1815

Grenadier of the 1st Regiment of Foot Guards in field service uniform, 1815

Grenadier of the 2nd Regiment of Foot Guards (Coldstream) in parade dress, 1815

Officer of the 3rd Regiment of Foot Guards (Scots Guards), 1815

Major-General, 1815

GREAT BRITAIN

Sharpshooter of the 95th Infantry Regiment (Rifle Corps), 1813

92nd Highland Infantry Regiment (Gordon Highlanders), 1813

Officer of the 97th (Queen's Own) Infantry Regiment, 1815

Infantryman of the 69th Infantry Regiment, 1812

Gunner of the Foot Artillery, 1814

GREAT BRITAIN

1st Regiment of Dragoon Guards ('King's Regiment')

Officer of the 2nd Regiment of the Life Guards in field service uniform, 1813

Guardsman of the 1st Regiment of Life Guards, 1815

Guardsman of the Horse Guards Regiment, 1815

Officer of the Mounted Artillery, 1815

GREAT BRITAIN

Officer of the 15th Regiment King's Light Dragoons (Hussars), 1815

Dragoon of the 3rd Light Dragoon Regiment, 1815

2nd or Royal North British Regiment of Dragoons (Scots Greys)

6th or Inniskilling 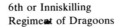 Regiment of Dragoons

2nd Heavy Dragoon Regiment

AUSTRIA

Grenadier of the 1st
(Emperor Francis II's)
German Infantry
Regiment, 1813

Infantryman of the 3rd
Archduke Charles's
German Infantry
Regiment, 1813

General, 1813

Officer of the Hoch- und
Deutschmeister German
Infantry Regiment, 1805

Grenadier of the 37th
Hungarian Infantry
Regiment, 1813

AUSTRIA

Austrian Territorial
Reserve, 1809

Artilleryman, 1815

Regimental Surgeon, 1811

Serbian Frey Battalion,
1813

Infantryman of the
German Legion, 1813

AUSTRIA

Trumpeter of the 4th
Dragoon Regiment (Grand
Duke of Tuscany's),
1813–15

Trooper of the 4th
(Windisch-Graetz's)
Regiment of Light Horse,
1813

Cuirassier of the 8th
Cuirassier Regiment
(Hohenzollern-Hechingen's),
1813

Dragoon of the 6th
(Ficquelmont's) Dragoon
Regiment, 1813

Uhlan of
Sachsen-Coburg-Saalfeld's
Regiment of Uhlans, 1815

AUSTRIA

Hussar of Szekler's Hussar
Regiment, 1813

Hussar of the
Hessen-Homburg Hussar
Regiment, 1813

Hussar of the Emperor's
Hussar Regiment, 1813

Hussar trumpeter of the
Archduke Joseph Anton's
Hussar Regiment, 1806

Hussar of the Frimont
Hussar Regiment, 1813

RUSSIA
Musketeer, 1809

Grenadier, 1812–15

Musketeer, 1805–6

Gunner of the Foot
Artillery, 1806–7

Mounted Artillery of the
Russo-German Legion,
1812–14

RUSSIA
Grenadier of the Pavlov
Guards Regiment

Chasseur Officer, 1809

General in summer parade
dress, 1808–9

Chasseur, 1814

Officer of the Territorial
Reserve, 1812–14

RUSSIA

Uhlan of Grand Duke
Nicholas's Regiment of
Uhlans, 1806

Dragoon of the Courland
Dragoon Regiment, 1813

Cuirassier of the Little
Russia Cuirassier
Regiment, 1814

Hussar of the Pavlovgrad
Hussar Regiment

NCO of the Seversk
Mounted Chasseur
Regiment

RUSSIA

Trooper of the 1st
Mounted Home Guard
Regiment of St Petersburg
Province, 1812

Cuirassier of the Horse
Guards Regiment,
1812–13

Officer of the Chevalier
Guards Regiment, 1812

Uhlan of the Guard
Uhlan Regiment, 1812

Cossack of the Imperial
Guard, 1812–14

NAPLES

Grenadier of the 1st
Guards Grenadier
Battalion

Fusilier of the 1st Line
Infantry Regiment

Musician of the 5th
Infantry Regiment, 1812

Adjutant, 1812

Grenadier Officer of the
7th 'Africa' Regiment,
1812

NAPLES

King's Orderly, 1812

Trooper of the Light
Horse Regiment, 1812

Officer of the Mounted
Chasseurs, 1812

Dragoon, 1812

Officer of the Guards
Hussar Regiment, 1812

SPAIN

Princesa' Infantry
Regiment, 1807,
Drum-Major (old uniform)

Grenadier, Princesa'
Infantry Regiment,
1806, 1808 (old uniform)

Officer of the Barcelona
Light Regiment, 1807,
1808

Light Infantryman of the
Line Infantry of the
Spanish National Army,
1812

Infantryman, Spanish
National Army, Patria
Infantry Regiment, 1808

SPAIN

8th 'Espania' Regiment of
Line Cavalry, 1806

Mounted Chasseur and
Chasseur, Almansa
Regiment, 1807 and 1808

Dragoon of the 'Pavia'
Dragoon Regiment, 1806

Hussar of Maria Luisa's
Hussar Regiment, 1806

Trooper of the Guards
Light Horse (under Joseph
Napoleon), 1809

NETHERLANDS
Grenadier of the 5th Infantry Regiment, 1806–10

Fusilier of the 3rd Infantry Regiment, 1806–10

Gunner of the Mounted Artillery, 1806–10

Chasseur, 1815

Infantryman, 1815

NETHERLANDS
Cuirassier of the 2nd Cuirassier Regiment, 1807–10

Hussar of the 2nd Hussar Regiment, 1807–10

Officer of the 5th Light Dragoon Regiment, 1815

Hussar of the 6th Hussar Regiment, 1815

Gunner of the Mounted Artillery, 1815

DENMARK

Trooper of the Holstein Mounted Regiment, 1802

Dragoon of the Fyen Light Dragoon Regiment, 1813

Officer of the Norwegian Leibregiment, 1807

Chasseur of the 'Leib' Chasseur Company, 1807

Infantryman of the Schleswig Infantry Regiment, 1813

SWEDEN

2nd Leibgarde Regiment, 1807

Officer of the Leibgrenadier Corps, 1807

Infantryman of the Södermannland Regiment, 1807

Musketeer in field service uniform, Queen's Leibregiment, 1807

Officer of the Leibkürassier Regiment, 1807

KINGDOM OF BAVARIA

Grenadier of the Crown
Prince's Regiment, 1809

Dragoon of the 1st
Dragoon Regiment, 1807

Officer of the King's
Regiment of Light Horse,
1811

Garde du corps Regiment,
1814

Royal Bavarian Grenadier
Guards Regiment, 1814

KINGDOM OF WESTPHALIA

Chasseur of the Guards
Chasseurs, 1812

Gunner of the Guards
Artillery

Officer of the 2nd
Cuirassier Regiment, 1812

Hussar of the 1st Hussar
Regiment

Grenadier of the 4th
Westphalian Infantry
Regiment in marching kit

SAXONY

Fusilier of Low's Infantry Regiment, 1813

Cuirassier of von Zastrow's Regiment, 1812

Hussar of the Hussar Regiment, 1806

Cuirassier of the Leibkürassier Guards, 1812

Prince Frederick Augustus' Infantry Regiment, 1806

WURTTEMBERG

1st Light Infantry Battalion (von Neubronn), 1806

Officer of the King's Mounted Chasseur Regiment, 1808

Officer of the Guards Mounted Chasseur Regiment, 1815

Trooper of the 2nd Leib Regiment of Light Horse, 1812

Infantryman of the 6th Regiment of Infantry (Crown Prince's), 1813

hussars were not greatly bothered by this. Up to the time of Waterloo they wore plumes of every colour, and even the trumpeters were distinguished by their bright shakos. Instead of monotonous black, they wore shakos of light blue (2nd, 9th and 10th Regiments), red (4th, 8th and 13th Regiments), white (5th Regiment), green (7th Regiment) and brown (13th and 14th Regiments).

Lastly, appearance was also determined by particular circumstances. In 1806, as a result of the British naval blockade, there was a shortage of the indigo used for dyeing cloth and so Napoleon ordered the introduction of a white uniform for his line infantry. Only eighteen of the 112 regiments were issued with these when, in 1807, the importing of indigo resumed and the blue uniforms were reinstated. However, in 1811 French infantrymen were still fighting in Spain in white uniforms, and when it was decided to issue new uniforms to the two French carabinier regiments at the end of 1809, Napoleon settled on madder-red as the basic colour. However, since this cloth was not available in sufficient quantity, while white was readily available, the regiments were given white uniforms contrary to the wishes of the Emperor.

It was the same story with head-dress. France may have introduced the shako in 1804, but in 1806 the French infantry was for the greater part still wearing the felt bicorne, and in 1812 the line grenadiers could still be seen wearing the busby which should have been discarded along with the felt hat. Existing stocks had still to be exhausted.

There was similar confusion in Prussia when war broke out in 1806, for at precisely this time new head-dress had been introduced. In theory the *Feldjäger* should have worn shakos, but in fact were still wearing hats. Shakos had likewise been prescribed for the hussars (in place of flugel caps), but they were being worn in only two of eleven regiments, and even there the trumpeters kept their traditional flugel caps. In 1806 officers of the Prussian hussars still appeared at times in long coats and hats, and the colour of the hussars' breeches was often left to chance, or rather to the state of the stores. For example, the Gettkandt Hussars should have worn white breeches with their dark green dolmans and pelisses, but they fought at the battle of Jena wearing red ones.

After the defeats of Jena and Auerstädt the situation in Prussia became even more confused. For new volunteer corps set up in Silesia, reserve supplies were used; from stocks of material for the uniforms of the 'Schimmelpfennig' Hussars (6th Regiment) von Losthin's Battalion of Grenadiers dressed in brown trousers and facings – a very unusual infantry uniform for Prussia up to that time. When there was a general shortage of uniforms in the new offensive against Napoleon in 1813, the members of the Lützow volunteer corps had the stocks of cloth dyed black. From the black uniform with red facings and gold buttons – a combination of three colours which German students adopted after 1815 – came the national colours of a democratic Germany in 1848: black–red–gold, the national colours of the Federal Republic of Germany after 1945.

The uniform as laid down was in practice worn with so many modifications that it is often difficult, and sometimes even impossible, to identify with certainty soldiers depicted in contemporary representations. And this is not only a problem for us today, but one that soldiers occasionally had to face in battle. Many of them must have perished because they could not be identified when necessary. A particularly striking example of this is recounted by the

KINGDOM OF ITALY
Italy under the Viceroy
Eugène Beauharnais, 1812,
Officer of the Guards
Foot Artillery

Carabinier of the Guards
Infantry Regiment, 1812

Dragoon of the Dragoon
Regiment of the Royal
Guard, 1812

DUCHY OF WARSAW
Light Infantryman of the
Line Infantry, 1812

Hussar of the 13th Hussar
Regiment, 1812

GERMAN STATES
Brunswick, Infantryman of
the Duke of Brunswick's
Corps, 1809

Anhalt, officer of the 5th
Infantry Regiment of the
Confederation of the
Rhine

Nassau, Officer of the
Mounted Chasseurs, 1807

Lippe, Infantryman, 1812

Brunswick, Hussar of the
Duke of Brunswick's
Corps, 1809

GERMAN STATES

Hessen-Darmstadt, Light
Horse, 1812

Hessen-Darmstadt,
Grenadier of the Crown
Prince's Regiment, 1809

*Grand Duchy of
Würzburg*, Dragoon, 1807

Saxony-Weimar,
Carabinier, 1812

Principality of Waldeck,
6th Infantry Regiment of
the Prince's Division, 1812

GRAND DUCHY OF BADEN

Infantryman of the
Leibregiment, 1812

Dragoon of the 1st
Dragoon Regiment, 1813

NCO of the Grand Duke's
Regiment, 1813

DUCHY OF CLEVE-BERG

Mounted Chasseur, 1812   Grenadier, 1812

The Dragoon Regiment of the Elector of Pfalz and Bayern encamped near Berlin in 1803. Painting by Carl W. Kolbe.

French General Marbot in his memoirs of the Battle of Fuentes de Onoro in Spain in 1811.

A battalion of the Hanoverian Legion, attached to the Ferey division, wore, as did the English, red jackets, but, like the remainder of the French infantry, grey overcoats. Recalling unpleasant experiences at Busaco, the battalion commander had asked permission before the battle began for his men to wear their coats, but Loison had refused the request. This led to an atrocious blunder, for the French 66th regiment, sent ahead to support the Hanoverians, took them for an English battalion and opened fire on them, while our artillery, deceived by their red jackets, showered them with grapeshot. When the unfortunate Hanoverians, with over 100 dead and still more wounded, retreated past the village, the soldiers of a French regiment who had at that very moment entered it, also misled by the red battledress, thought they were out-flanked. As a result, such confusion arose that the enemy succeeded in retaking Fuentes de Onoro.

And this was not an isolated incident: in the battle of Wagram (1809) the Saxon infantry under the command of Marshal Bernadotte was fired upon by its French allies, because the French had confused the white uniform of the Saxons, which had red facings, with the almost identical uniform of their Austrian adversaries. And at Waterloo (1815) the troops of Nassau were fired upon by their Prussian allies because they were still wearing the old French-style uniforms, albeit dyed.

In Spain, in 1811, a piquet of the British Light Dragoons was captured, because it had mistaken the approaching enemy for hussars of the King's German Legion, and the Duke of Wellington raged: 'At a distance, or in action, colours are good for nothing: the profile, and shape of the man's cap and his general appearance are what guide us. And why should we make our people look like the French?' But Wellington also admitted: 'There is no subject of which I understand so little.' For him, it seems in fact to have been a matter of complete indifference how a soldier was dressed.

He shared this opinion with his opponent Napoleon. The great emperor, although himself the creator of the most colourful and flamboyant army of all time, was simply bored by questions of uniform. It is true that in 1816, on St Helena, he criticized his adjutant Gourgaud for wearing red riding-breeches – 'I do not care for this colour – it is the colour the English wear!' But in 1810 he had his 2nd regiment of *garde-lanciers* dressed in scarlet uniforms, and in 1809 the carabiniers should also have been given a red uniform. That Napoleon was not insensitive to the appearance of a well turned-out troop of soldiers is shown by his cry at Waterloo, when he caught sight of Wellington's Scots Greys, a Scottish dragoon regiment mounted on grey horses: *'Qui sont ces beaux cavaliers?'* He himself, though, always wore a very simple uniform

– as a matter of style and in emulation of his hero Frederick II of Prussia – but thought it important that his surroundings should appear all the more splendid, since an elaborate setting emphasized his own simplicity.

With the exception of Alexander I of Russia, who is said to have been personally responsible for creating the Russian shako (known as the *kiwer*), a shako whose front and back were cocked, and which was worn by the Russian infantry from 1812 onwards, only one monarch of the time showed any interest in uniforms. This was Frederick-William III of Prussia, who was contemptuously described by a member of his own House, Prince Louis Ferdinand of Prussia, as a 'military tailor'. Only a few weeks before the collapse of Prussia in 1807 he was preoccupied with the provision of a new uniform for his army, when in fact the army hardly existed and the state coffers were empty. At the Tilsit negotiations he could think of no better way to please his conqueror Napoleon than to regale him with detailed information about uniforms. Nine years later, Napoleon commented mordantly, 'I failed to understand a single word of this trivia.'

As late as 1814, the Prussian king refused to allow the Yorck Army Corps to participate in the Paris victory parade because he thought that the troops were of 'poor appearance' with their torn uniforms. But the majority of soldiers in the Napoleonic wars were of 'poor appearance'. The colours used for dyeing cloth faded rapidly, while sun, rain and dirt soon made uniforms unsightly. The splendid colours of contemporary battle scenes are misleading; in reality the colours of most scenes of carnage must have been a dirty grey-brown. General Marbot, quoted above, gives this report of an episode during the battle of Hanau (1813):

'The Battle of Chiclana,
5 March 1811' by Louis
Francois Lejeune.

We drove the Austrian Ott Hussar regiment before us in flight. I never saw finer hussars. They had come straight from Vienna and were in brand new uniforms. Their dress made a somewhat theatrical, but at the same time glittering impression. It consisted of short pelisses, white dolmans with dark red overalls and head-dress of the same colour. Everything about them was so bright and shining that they were a delightful sight. You might have thought that they were on their way back from a ball or a masque. This gleaming outfit was in sharp contrast to the more than modest clothing of my chasseurs, many of whom were still using the worn-out garments in which they had been bivouacked for a year and a half in Russia, Poland and Germany, and whose colours had become unrecognizable under the powder smoke and dust of battlefields. But beneath these shabby uniforms beat the undismayed, courageous hearts of strong men. After our pursuit, the magnificent white pelisses no longer looked so fine, for they were soon stained with blood.

On the other hand, not all battle scenes can have been idealized for in many battles the soldiers did in fact fight in dress uniform. For example at Borodino (1812), Napoleon specifically ordered the wearing of the *grande tenue* to give the soldiers the sense of participating in a festive occasion.

Uniforms were expensive, and officers had to pay for them out of their own pocket. The uniform of a French infantryman of the guard cost 258 francs, while the cavalryman paid as much as 517 francs. In total, between 1806 and 1810, the French state had to pay the sum of 20,000,000 francs, enormous by contemporary standards, for the uniforms of the *Garde Impériale*. Even more expensive was the uniform of the front line carabiniers, which included a copper cuirass set with brass plates and a matching helmet (partly inlaid with silver in the case of officers): this cost 2,000 francs.

After the end of the Napoleonic era – that is, after 1815 – uniforms became altogether plainer, although luxuries such as tiger-skin saddle-cloths and leopard-skin helmet trimmings (which had been introduced as early as the eighteenth century) survived. However, the states whose funds were exhausted as a result of the protracted and costly wars now reduced expenditure on uniform and cut down their armies to save money.

Yet up to the middle of the nineteenth century, military fashions remained in many ways indebted to models of the Napoleonic period. The veterans of this epoch, writing their memoirs in their old age, occasionally mourned the passage of such magnificent uniforms. They consoled themselves with the conviction that no greater military splendour, bound up as it was with the charisma of their emperor, had ever been seen in Europe, or would ever be seen again. And when Napoleon's body was transferred to the Hôtel des Invalides in Paris on 15 December 1840, the golden catafalque was followed by a troop of elderly men: these were the last survivors of Napoleon's *Grande Armée*, and all wore their old, long-faded and tattered uniforms.

Britain's Colonial Wars in the Nineteenth Century 5

MICHAEL BARTHORP

GREAT BRITAIN
Private, 17th Light
Dragoons, Pindari Wars,
India, 1816–17

Corporal, Light Company
of the 14th Regiment of
Foot (Siege of Bhurtpore,
India, 1825–26)

Officer of the 2nd
Regiment of Foot (First
Afghan War, 1839–42)

Private, Grenadier
Company of the 17th
Regiment of Foot (First
Afghan War, 1839–42)

Officer of the 3rd Light
Dragoons (King's Own) –
Sikh Wars, 1845–6

GREAT BRITAIN
Private, Battalion
Company of the 23rd
Regiment of Foot (Sikh
Wars, 1845–6, 1848,
1849)

60th King's Royal Rifle
Corps (Sikh Wars,
1848–9)

Corporal of the 6th
Regiment of Foot (8th
Kaffir War, South Africa,
1850–3)

Private of the 74th
(Highland) Regiment of
Foot (8th Kaffir War,
South Africa, 1850–3)

Private, 52nd Light
Infantry (Indian Mutiny,
1857–9)

GREAT BRITAIN

Private of the 7th (Queen's Own) Light Dragoons (Hussars), Indian Mutiny 1857–9

Sergeant, 4th Regiment of Foot (3rd China War, 1860)

Private of the 68th Light Infantry (3rd Maori War, New Zealand, 1864–6)

Private of the 4th Regiment of Foot (Abyssinian War, 1868)

Officer of the 42nd (Royal Highland) Regiment of Foot, Ashanti War, 1873–4

GREAT BRITAIN

Private of the 67th Regiment of Foot (2nd Afghan War, 1878)

Officer of the 58th Regiment of Foot (Zulu War, 1879, and 1st Boer War, 1881)

Private of the Heavy Camel Regiment (Life Guards), Sudan Campaign, 1884–5

Private of the Grenadier Guards (Reconquest of the Sudan, 1898

Officer (Boer War, 1899–1902)

The end of the Napoleonic Wars found most of the British army dressed in uniforms that were, by current standards, both serviceable and comfortable. During the occupation of Paris, however, it was soon realized that, compared with his allies, the British soldier cut a somewhat mean and shoddy figure, so, with the enthusiastic co-operation of that arch military milliner the Prince Regent, urgent measures were taken to smarten him up. Head-dresses grew in height and weight, in imitation of Continental models, gold lace proliferated, the easy-fitting, short-tailed jackets of the Peninsular War had their seams drawn in and their tails lengthened, and the sensible grey trousers were, some years later, replaced by garments of dark Oxford mixture or white, according to season. At the time, the banishment of Napoleon seemed to usher in a long period of peace, wherein the soldier's chief function would be one of display, and therefore the more resplendent he was the better.

While this may have suited most Continental armies, for the British the year 1816 saw the beginning of nearly nine decades of almost continual conflict across the world, usually on difficult terrain in oppressive climates, and against foes who, though often little more than savages by European standards, were frequently both formidable and numerous. Despite the countless military operations necessary to build and defend a great empire with a small all-volunteer army, very little thought was given by the military authorities in Britain to the problem of dressing and equipping the soldier for fighting rather than for parade, and broadly speaking the clothing and accoutrements laid down by regulations for home service were considered, by those authorities, equally appropriate for a winter skirmish in Canada, a punitive expedition in Afghanistan, or forest fighting in New Zealand.

Between 1816 and 1825 the British army fought a number of campaigns in India and Burma, but the only concessions to fighting in the tropics were the wearing of oilskin covers on the Prussian-type shakos of the infantry and the provision of light-weight trousers of local manufacture. A series of prints after drawings by eyewitnesses show the British infantry storming the stockades at Rangoon in 1825 wearing the same red coats as had been worn in Europe after Waterloo.

In 1829–30, largely for reasons of economy, the army's dress was modified slightly, but the lot of the infantry, the chief workhorses of the colonial wars, was but little eased for, instead of the Prussian shako, they received an equally top-heavy, bell-topped pattern, and the long-tailed coat was exchanged for a similar, but plainer garment, still with long tails, known as the coatee; this was to survive until 1855, some fifteen years after Continental armies had begun to adopt the full-skirted tunic. Cavalry uniforms lost some of their gold lace, but their head-dresses continued to be imposing and highly impractical.

Dressed thus, the army embarked on the first major campaign of Queen Victoria's reign, the First Afghan War of 1839–42. The troops suffered extremes of heat and cold in the most inhospitable terrain, yet apart from black or white covers for their shakos, they were dressed as for a review in England. The British officer has always been noted for his indifference to regulations regarding dress, particularly in the field, and, as early as the Burma War of 1825, no doubt conscious of the enormous expense and discomfort of his elaborate dress uniform, he preferred to campaign in his undress of forage cap and dark blue frock coat, later replaced by the shell

Men of the 13th (1st Somersetshire) Light Infantry regiment and Shah Shujah's Irregular horse during a sortie made from the besieged town of Jellālābād in the First Afghan War, 1839–42. The 13th are in forage caps and shell jackets or shirt-sleeves. Detail of a painting by David Cunliffe.

ABOVE The last stand of the 24th Regiment at the Battle of Isandhlwana, 22 January 1879, in the Zulu War. Painting by C. E. Fripp.

OPPOSITE 'The Battle of Meanee, 17 February 1843' by Edward Armitage RA. The 22nd (Cheshire) Regiment, seen in the foreground, and three regiments of Bombay Native Infantry defeated the Baluchis during the Conquest of Scinde by Sir Charles Napier, who appears in the background with arm outstretched.

The 16th (The Queen's) Lancers charging the Sikhs at the Battle of Aliwal, 28 January 1846. All ranks wear white-covered lancer caps, the officers scarlet stable jackets and the men dress jackets. Lithograph by Laby and Ogg after C. B. Spalding.

jacket: this was a plain, waist-length garment of red cloth, with collar and cuffs in the regimental facing colour and no tails. After 1830, when soldiers were also issued with shell jackets, the more enlightened commanding officers of regiments often allowed their men to wear these, with forage caps, on service; for a full field action the coatee was deemed more appropriate.

During the Sikh Wars of 1845–7 and 1848–9, the nearest approach to European warfare since Waterloo, as the Sikh army was trained and organized on European lines by European officers, British regiments appeared in a mixture of dress and undress uniform. At the Battle of Chillianwallah, for example, an officer noted:

'The 24th Regiment went into action in full dress with the inconvenient tall shako. The 29th were in undress jackets and forage caps. Some officers wore their blue frock coats, some dark trousers and shell jackets, and others long red or blue cotton coats, quilted, with turbans wound round their forage caps.' The 9th Regiment preferred a mixed dress, wearing shell jackets but with white-covered shakos. These were now of a cylindrical pattern with front and back peaks, which had been introduced in 1844 and known as the 'Albert', after the Prince Consort, who had had a hand in the design. The Light Dragoon and Lancer regiments affected a similar variety of dress, their shakos, or lancer caps, being fitted with quilted covers and the men wearing their dress jackets while the officers appeared in undress. The unpopularity of the full dress headgear was noted by a private of the 14th Light Dragoons who observed: 'Most of the men managed to lose their shakos before long and we often wore a towel soaked in water round the head, like a turban.'

While part of the British army campaigned in India, other regiments had been engaged in a number of little wars in southern Africa between 1835 and 1853, both against the Boers and rebellious tribes on the eastern frontier of Cape Colony. Here, with the experience of European settler pioneers to draw upon, regiments were quicker to adapt their regulation clothing for bush warfare. The coatees were docked of their non-functional embellishments and shell jackets were patched and reinforced with leather; broad peaks were fitted to the forage caps, although these were often discarded in favour of stocking caps or broad-brimmed felt or straw hats known as 'wide-awakes'; and a variety of trousers, brown or grey, buckskin or moleskin, were worn instead of the regulation pattern. The heavy black knapsacks and pipe-clayed cross-belts were replaced by lighter accoutrements, manufactured locally of untanned leather.

Many officers hardly bothered with uniform at all and fitted themselves out for the bush from the stores of the frontier townships. A subaltern was described as wearing:

a green wideawake, a frontier jacket, any colour you like, with lots of pockets, a pink flannel shirt, mimosa-stained corduroys of a faint purple colour and 'veldt' shoes of undressed leather; his weapons a double-barrelled gun and a Colt revolver; a leather strap buckled round the body supporting a large sealskin pouch for bullets and cartridges with a small one for caps. A leather side bag of jackal's hide, strapped on the saddle; a cloak or greatcoat rolled up in front of him and a tin pot adorns the horse's crupper.

The most revolutionary costume was that of the 74th Highlanders who, in 1851, discarded their red coatees in favour of canvas smocks dyed a brownish–grey–purple colour, which were worn with their tartan trews and forage caps fitted with a broad leather peak. They carried their blankets and greatcoats folded together to form a pack, to which the mess-tin was secured, and their belts, pouches and boots were all of untanned leather. This costume is the first appearance among British troops of a khaki-type uniform, but its adoption was for reasons of serviceability rather than the need for camouflage, a factor of less significance in those days of short-range firearms, although in bush-fighting concealment was a necessary adjunct to surprise. It might be mentioned here that the British soldier's red coat did not offer such an obvious target as might be thought, since the red was of a dull shade which, after exposure to the weather, attained a hue little different from shades of brown.

By the outbreak of the Crimean War in 1854, it had become more or less customary for the soldier to fight in his undress uniform, although this practice and the lessons learned in South Africa were not considered applicable to warfare against a European power and the British army went out to fight once more in its full dress, which by now was of a somewhat old-fashioned appearance compared with the uniforms of other Continental armies. In fact, the British authorities had decided, in 1854, to introduce the tunic, but the new dress did not begin to reach the troops until well into 1855–6. Other developments followed, for the British army's next campaign, the Indian Mutiny of 1857–9, saw the first adoption of khaki on a wide scale.

Khaki, so-called after a Hindustani word *khak* meaning dust, had first appeared in India in 1846 when Harry Lumsden, an officer of the Honourable East India Company's forces, had put his regiment, the Corps of Guides, into loose, mud-coloured blouses and pantaloons made of cotton, instead of the British-type uniforms worn by other native regiments. This sensible measure was not followed by either the Queen's or the Company's regiments until the outbreak of the Mutiny, which occurred during the hot weather, a time of year in which hitherto little campaigning had been conducted in the East.

The first British regiment to adopt khaki was the 52nd Light Infantry which, when ordered to the Siege of Delhi in May 1857, had all its white clothing, the usual uniform for summer, dyed in the local bazaar. The shade thus produced was 'the colour of the ground', to quote Bugler Johnson of the regiment, who further recalled that: 'Instead of the [white] shell jacket, nearly all wore the loose flannel shirt [also dyed] outside the trousers, with waist turban and belts outside. Our head-dress consisted of the old forage cap with khaki cover, curtain and puggaree [turban].' At about the same time the 61st Regiment had its white clothing dyed 'a sort of bluish brown colour'. The example of these two regiments was soon followed by the rest of the force at Delhi and before long it spread to the other areas of operations in India. European civilians were so accustomed to the sight of British soldiers in their smart, well-cut red or white uniforms, that when they first observed the battle-stained troops in loose-fitting, dirt-coloured clothing, they could not believe they were from European regiments and thought they must be the newly-raised native units from the Punjab.

With the onset of the cool weather, many of the khaki-clad regiments reverted to their cloth winter uniforms in the traditional colours. Regiments new to India, which came out as reinforcements from England, had to fight in their home service clothing, even in the hottest months, until they could obtain some form of khaki. The 2nd Dragoon Guards, for example, went into action at Lucknow in March 1858 wearing their scarlet tunics and brass helmets looking, according to an eyewitness, Lieutenant Majendie, 'as if they had come out for the express purpose of catching the rays of the sun'. A few regiments, which were diverted to India while *en route* from England to China, were rather better off as they had been issued with brown holland tunics with red facings, for wear when working boats up the Chinese rivers. The 93rd Highlanders wore these brown coats throughout the Mutiny, complete with their feather bonnets, to which a quilted peak or shade was attached, kilts, sporrans, hose and gaiters. The diversity of different regimental costumes made a colourful sight at the taking of Lucknow in 1858: 'Plumes of Highlanders waving gaily, dark coats of the Riflemen, the red uniforms of the Royal Welsh Fusiliers, the blue of the [European] Bengal Fusiliers and the artillery, and the serviceable karkee-coloured [sic] vestments of the Sikh Infantry.'

Towards the end of the Mutiny, most of the regiments engaged in operations had acquired khaki clothing of some sort. Since the methods of dyeing cotton were rudimentary in the extreme – the use of mud, tea-leaves, coffee and coloured inks are all recorded – the resulting colours varied between brown, slate, lavender and off-white. On their heads the troops wore either the old forage cap swathed in a turban, the so-called 'French' shako of the 1855 pattern with a cotton cover, or a new head-dress which quickly became popular, the sun helmet. Initially these were made of quilted cotton stretched over a wicker frame with a puggaree wrapped around and had an air vent in the form of a crest; subsequently pith or felt was used. To begin with, only officers had these helmets but, as the campaign progressed, they began to reach all ranks.

Despite the widespread use of khaki during the Mutiny, no attempt was made thereafter to adopt a regulation khaki uniform for active service. A simplified, easy-fitting version of the full dress cloth tunic, made of loosely woven serge in the traditional colours and known as a frock, replaced the shell jacket as the soldier's undress uniform and became the customary garment for service. Although the force engaged in the campaign in China in 1860 had been issued with khaki suits, these were ordered to be packed in the knapsacks and the troops fought in their red serge frocks, cloth trousers and either covered forage caps or wicker helmets. A similar costume prevailed during the Umbeyla expedition on the North-West Frontier of India in 1863.

On the other hand, for the operations against the Maoris in New Zealand at the same period, the infantry were fitted out with blue frocks, which were thought to be more suitable for forest fighting than the red ones. During the First Maori War of 1845–7 red shell jackets had been worn, but when trouble broke out again in 1860, the troops took the field wearing their dark grey greatcoats with the skirts cut short. However, this proved unsatisfactory, hence the adoption of the blue frocks which were worn with the dark cloth trousers. Helmets were not issued in New Zealand and the men made do with the forage cap; this was still the round pattern with a tuft on top, now worn a little lower than those originally introduced in 1834, but still basically the same cap of dark blue knitted wool, or dark green for light infantry and rifles, and bearing the regimental number in brass on the front; those of officers and sergeants were blocked out and were fitted

Typical Indian Mutiny infantrymen at Cawnpore in 1857 in grey-buff smocks; the right-hand soldier wears the 1855 shako in a grey cover. Lithograph after Lieutenant Sankey, Madras Engineers.

Men of the 71st Highlands Light Infantry as they appeared during the Umbeyla Expedition on the North-West Frontier of India in 1863. The men's coats are the first pattern of red serge frock and the sprigs of fir in the forage caps denote the regimental sharpshooters.

with a flat peak. The normal accoutrements of pouch belt, waist-belt with bayonet frog, and haversack were carried and the blanket or greatcoat was folded into a long roll and slung over the left shoulder, a fashion that had started in the Indian Mutiny.

In 1868 an expeditionary force was sent from India against the mad Emperor of Abyssinia, Theodore, who was holding a number of Europeans captive. This was the first campaign in which khaki was worn outside India, although the khaki clothing was simply the white summer uniforms which were hurriedly dyed before the force sailed. According to the watercolours of an officer who was present, the khaki thus produced was of a greyish shade. The men had their red frocks with them to wear when the weather got cold, and some units even wore them in action, as can be seen in this eyewitness description of the force's diversified appearance: 'It was a fine sight to see the long line of red, Royal Engineers (toiling under their scaling ladders), 33rd and 45th Regiments, the 4th King's Own in their grey karkee [sic], the Beloochees [27th Bombay Native Infantry] in their dark green, the Royal Artillery in blue.' Although the reference to the 'long line' implies that the 33rd, as well as the Royal Engineers, were dressed in red on this occasion, at the storming of Magdala which ended the campaign, this regiment, accord-ing to the above-mentioned watercolours, wore grey khaki; the Engineers however were still in red. All ranks had the crested sun helmets, and the campaign witnessed two innovations: the use by the British infantry of their first breech-loading rifle, the Snider-Enfield, and the wearing of short black leather gaiters. Since the Napoleonic Wars British soldiers had worn their trousers ungathered at the ankle, which naturally caused much fraying and tearing, and although these gaiters had been intro-duced nine years before, the Abyssinian campaign was the first occasion when they were used on active service.

An officer and men of the 4th (King's Own) Regiment after the capture of Magdala, Abyssinia, 1868. This photograph shows the crested helmets and khaki-dyed white Indian summer uniforms worn during this campaign.

Unlike the pre-Crimean period, when a relaxed attitude to the soldier's fighting dress was more evident in South Africa than elsewhere, since 1855 all the evolutions towards a more practical battledress had emanated from India. However, in 1873, a force under that great military reformer, Sir Garnet Wolseley, left England for an expedition against the Ashanti tribe of West Africa in a uniform specially designed for the campaign. A new tropical helmet was issued, made of cork and canvas with a puggaree wrapped round it, but without the crested air vent, which had already been removed from the helmets worn in India. Each man received two suits of clothing, consisting of a frock and trousers of Elcho grey tweed, which were worn with canvas gaiters, slightly longer than the regulation black leather pattern. The *Illustrated London News* said of the frock that it introduced 'a novelty into the uniform of the Army, in the shape of outside pockets, of which there are three, one on each hip and one on the left breast. The garment fits loosely about the neck and chest, it is confined at the waist by a belt of its own material, there is no stiffness in the collar and it is a comfortable and serviceable dress'. With this costume, the troops wore the newly designed Valise Pattern Equipment, which abolished the old ammunition pouch, or cartouche box, slung over the left shoulder, which had been in use in various designs since the eighteenth century, in favour of two smaller pouches and an expense pouch, or ball bag, all fitted on the waist-belt. The big, rectangular knapsack was replaced by a valise, the weight of which was more evenly spread across the back and hips, although in colonial campaigning these would normally be carried on transport, as had been the knapsacks. Buff leather was used for the belt, straps and, in some issues, the pouches; in others,

the latter were of black leather, as were the valise and ball bag, although the material used for the last two items was more pliable. Finally a new water bottle, the Oliver, or Italian pattern, superseded the old, wooden, circular keg type. A special, long bayonet with a swelling spear point and saw-backed blade was issued for this campaign and was also carried by officers instead of their swords; in addition, officers of the 42nd Highlanders armed themselves with Snider carbines.

Despite the increased comfort and practicality afforded by this new dress, once again the opportunity was lost and no attempt was made, after the Ashanti War, to adopt it, or something similar, as the British army's fighting kit. Indeed, the soldier's serge frock had by now been smartened up, with shorter skirts and regimental facings and collar badges added; except for the number of buttons, it could scarcely be distinguished from the man's cloth tunic. In the Zulu War of 1879 and the First Boer War of 1881 the troops again fought in their traditional coloured frocks, dark trousers and black leather gaiters. Although the white helmets, which in South Africa at this period were worn without puggarees, and the accoutrements were stained brown, the Boers found the scarlet coats of the British infantry an easy target and an incomprehensible colour for fighting in, now that the long-range, breech-loading rifle was in common use. Officers by now had the choice of two undress jackets, one scarlet, the other blue. During these two campaigns some officers, particularly those on the staff, preferred to wear the blue, and it was to this choice that one officer believed he owed his life after the disaster at Isandhlwana in the Zulu War, since the Zulu king, Cetshwayo, had informed his warriors that the soldiers could be identified from civilians by their red coats.

Officers and men of the
1st Life Guards and
Grenadier Guards dressed
for the Egyptian Campaign
of 1882. Note the valise
equipment of the grenadier
and the sun goggles and
face veils. Engraving by
W. H. Overend.

Meanwhile the British army in India had been engaged in the Second Afghan War of 1878–80. The white summer uniforms were again dyed and some regiments received a garment somewhat resembling a Norfolk jacket which, in the bitter cold of the Afghan winter, the troops wore over their scarlet frocks with the dark, home service trousers, which had now changed in colour to a very dark blue. The headgear, whatever the weather, was the white Indian helmet fitted with a khaki cover; this was exchanged at night or when off-duty for the forage cap, a dark blue Glengarry for the infantry, which had replaced the round, 'pork-pie' type, or the pill-box pattern for the cavalry. Two other fashions, which subsequently would be adopted by armies all over the world, became popular during this campaign: first, the wearing of puttees, khaki for infantry, dark blue for cavalry and artillery, which were thought to give more support to the leg than gaiters, and second, the carriage of the officer's sword and revolver on the brown leather belt and brace named after its inventor, Sam Browne, an old Mutiny officer of Indian cavalry. Towards the end of this war, a permanently-dyed khaki uniform was devised and thereafter an all-khaki turnout, helmet, frock, trousers and puttees, became the regulation dress for all later campaigns in India and Burma.

For the British army outside India, the serge frock remained the soldier's campaign jacket. Wolseley's army, which defeated Arabi Pasha at the victory of Tel-el-Kebir in Egypt in 1882, was so dressed, with brown-stained helmets, blue trousers and leather gaiters. While observers of the campaign noted that the scarlet coats were less conspicuous in the desert at a distance than the white uniforms of the Egyptian army, they also drew a less favourable comparison between the grimy, sweat-stained

The charge of the 21st Lancers at the Battle of Omdurman in the Sudan, 1898. The officers are wearing the new Wolseley pattern helmets. Painting by R. Cato-Woodville.

An officer of the Queen's Own Cameron Highlanders during the Reconquest of the Sudan in 1898. The officer is wearing the Wolseley pattern helmet, and the soldiers have Slade-Wallace equipment.

scarlet and the cool, practical khaki worn by the small contingent sent from India.

The advantages of khaki were now beginning to be grasped by the military authorities in England, and for the campaigns in the Sudan from 1884–5 to quell the Dervishes and relieve General Gordon besieged in Khartoum, the troops were first issued with a grey serge uniform which, in the latter stages of the fighting, was changed for khaki cotton drill of a sandy colour. Puttees were worn by mounted troops and by some of the infantry which came from India; those regiments from England wore their trousers loose. Nevertheless, there were still those who favoured the old scarlet, particularly against savage enemies, and, at the last battle of the Sudan campaign at Ginniss in 1885, some of the regiments were ordered to put on their scarlet frocks above their khaki trousers, to render them more formidable in the eyes of the Dervishes.

In the few military operations that had occurred in Canada during the reign of Queen Victoria, the rebellion of 1837–9, the Fenian Raids of 1866 and the Red River Expedition of 1870, clothing of the home service pattern had been worn by British regulars and Canadian militia. Now, while khaki was supplanting red in the eastern hemisphere, the uprising of Louis Riel in 1885 was put down by Canadian regiments wearing the scarlet or green uniforms of the British infantry, some even displaying the latter's blue cloth, spiked helmet, which had been introduced for home service after the Franco-Prussian War of 1870, in imitation of the victor's head-dress; despite its long life as the British infantryman's headgear, Riel's rebellion was the only occasion when it was worn on field service.

The last time when the traditional colours were worn in action by British troops is thought to have been during an uprising in Zululand in 1888 when the 6th Dragoons and the Royal Scots took the field in blue and red frocks respectively, although the mounted infantry company of the latter regiment were more comfortably dressed in blue jerseys. As late as 1896 a small force, made up of detachments from various regiments in England and wearing serge frocks, blue trousers and the canvas gaiters issued for the 1873 campaign against the Ashantis, was sent to quell the same tribe, but no fighting actually occurred.

At home in the eighties and nineties, garments in the traditional colours were still regulation for training and manoeuvres. An experimental field uniform, of a colour described as 'a warm drab-grey', had been devised in early 1884 and issued to one or two regiments in England, but it had not proved popular, the scarlet coat having a strong appeal for its wearers, who feared its permanent departure. The new uniform also had a number of defects of design, so consequently the proposal was dropped. It was not until 1896, when the problems of producing a satisfactory and permanent khaki dye were solved, that such a uniform was finally authorized as the regulation dress for all foreign service, but not for troops at home.

The army with which Lord Kitchener reconquered the Sudan in 1898 was entirely dressed in khaki, except for the Highland regiments who retained their kilts and diced hose. A corporal in the Seaforth Highlanders wrote home:

We are here in very light order. We march with straps, pouches, haversacks and large water bottles. We carry on our person 100 rounds in the pouches and 20 in the haversack. Our blankets are carried on camels and our kit-bags, valises, and greatcoats are on boats on the Nile, so that we have only our clothes as we stand. Before we left Cairo we were each provided with a back pad for protecting the spine, which we always wear (the khaki coat not keeping out the heat well), shade for the back of the neck, attached to the helmet, mosquito veil, goggles, useful for glare and sand-storms, knitted night cap, also very comfortable. We wear khaki spats and helmet covers, and each regiment has a distinguishing badge in the helmet. The others wear a small square of coloured cloth, but we are resplendent with tartan [square], badge and hackle!

The infantry had a new set of accoutrements, the Slade-Wallace pattern which, though still made of buff leather, offered some improvements on the previous design, and a magazine rifle, the Lee-Metford which, in 1888, had replaced the single-loading Martini-Henry, in use since 1874. The only cavalry regiment engaged, the 21st Lancers, were dressed like the infantry, except for breeches instead of trousers, and were armed with sword, lance and carbine, carrying their ammunition in a leather bandolier, fitted with loops in five groups of ten, which had first seen service with the Camel Corps, formed to relieve Gordon in 1884. This campaign also saw the first appearance, though worn only by officers, of a new type of sun helmet, the Wolseley pattern, which had a flatter brim and which would later become the regulation helmet, but not until around 1905 since, as will be seen, an entirely different head-dress would achieve popularity in the interim.

When war with the Boers broke out again in 1899, the large force that was despatched was dressed and accoutred exactly as for the Sudan campaign, although the Highlanders now had khaki kilt aprons and not all regiments used the neck shades for the helmets. As a result, the Boers found the British soldier a much less conspicuous target than he had been in 1881. To avoid being picked off by enemy marksmen, regimental officers retained the same helmet as their men and quickly gave up their swords for rifles. As the war progressed the khaki cotton drill was found to be insufficiently hard-wearing and not warm enough, so khaki serge began to be issued instead. The old helmet, with its steeply sloping brim, proved to be inconvenient when firing from the prone position so, emulating the fashion of the South African, Australian and New Zealand contingents, many British officers and men adopted the broad-brimmed felt, or 'slouch' hat, which afforded a lighter and more practical alternative. Nevertheless the helmet was still to be seen in large numbers up until the end of the war in 1902; some officers considered the hat to be unsmart and forbade its use in their units.

The twin pouches of the equipment were also found to be unsatisfactory since they did not permit sufficient ammunition to be carried and the rounds tended to fall out when the man lay down to fire. Some of the infantry adopted the cavalry bandolier as an additional ammunition carrier until a new type of bandolier, made of webbing and holding 100 rounds, was introduced. These were loosely woven and intended to be expendable, but the soldiers liked to retain them, wearing them both round the waist and over the shoulder. However, since they were cheaply made, the cartridge loops expanded with constant use and failed to grip the rounds tightly. It is said that one of the reasons that enabled the Boers to fight on so long during the guerrilla fighting of 1901–2 was the quantity of ammunition they managed to pick up which had been dropped by British soldiers.

After the war, the faults in the soldier's dress and equipment which had been revealed were seriously studied and acted upon. A khaki serge uniform of a darker hue became the soldier's dress for all save full dress occasions, at home as well as abroad. For a few years the slouch hat was the official campaign headgear and a new bandolier equipment, made of leather, replaced the Slade-Wallace type. By 1908 these too had given way to the peaked khaki cap and a novel design of webbing equipment, which all fitted together in one assembly. For almost the first time, the design of the soldier's dress for battle was considered scientifically and to such good effect that, when war broke out in 1914, the British soldier was the most sensibly dressed and accoutred fighting man in Europe.

The Rise of the Mass Armies
1815-60

6

JOHN MOLLO

After 1815 the armies of Europe were all, at one time or another, employed on what are now called 'internal security' duties for which a small and reliable professional army was the first requirement. However, the lurking fear of a minor incident getting out of hand led both Russia and Austria to maintain large and potentially unreliable armies. The Prussian army, for reasons of economy, was less menacing, while the French army languished in isolation, hated by the proletariat and shunned by the comfort-loving bourgeoisie.

The social and political struggles of the period were reflected in the dress of the participants as the influence of one or other great power spread to its allies and dependants. In particular the occupation of Paris in 1814, and again in 1815, provided a melting-pot of sartorial ideas. The British and Russians both abandoned their distinctive head-dress in favour of the bell-topped shako worn by the French, Prussians and Austrians; the Prussians adopted the long all-in-one overalls of the Russians, and gradually all their uniforms became stiffer and tighter. Portugal, some of the newly formed South American states and the USA were influenced by Britain, the Italian states by Austria, the German states partly by Prussia and partly by Austria, while the Prussians aped the fashions of St Petersburg. In the years before 1830 military fashions were also set by the various European monarchs, who, as never before or since, allowed their imaginations free rein.

After 1830, with cracks appearing in the solid façade of the Holy Alliance, a wave of romanticism swept through the field of military costume. In the early 1840s the celebrated spiked helmet, the *pickelhaube*, first made its appearance, both Russia and Prussia claiming the original idea. By 1848 uniforms had acquired definite political implications, the stiff Russian and Prussian uniforms becoming synonymous with repression, while the looser French style became the symbol of liberty to patriots everywhere.

The Russian army, some 800,000 strong, was the largest and most imposing army in the world, but beneath its glittering surface there were serious defects which all the efforts of Nicholas I failed to eradicate, in spite of continuous active service against the Persians in 1826, the Turks in 1828, the Poles in 1831, the Hungarians in 1849, and finally the British, French and Sardinians in the Crimea, quite apart from thirty years of continuous warfare in the Caucasus.

Under the leaden gaze of an Emperor never seen in public except crammed into a creaseless uniform, the Russian army achieved a standard of 'spit and polish' probably never surpassed. Nevertheless Russian uniforms were simple in design, and of an extreme uniformity. Although the cut was exaggerated, the stuffs used were very coarse. The soldiers made their own shirts, boots and underwear; uniforms and greatcoats were made in the regiment; and head-dress and equipment were issued by the government, usually once every ten years. Examples of uniforms of the period reveal minute darns and repairs, mute testimony to the husbandry of the Russian private soldier.

After 1815 the Russians abandoned the characteristic *kiwer*, and adopted the tall shako of French form, which was worn, with minor modifications, by the infantry, dragoons, *chevau-légers*, hussars and artillery until the advent of the spiked helmet in 1844. There were several changes of shako plate which by 1828 had resolved themselves into two patterns, the complete double-headed eagle which was worn by the guards, and the Amazon shield surmounted

by a double-headed eagle, which was worn by the line. Both plates survived the change to the spiked helmet and were worn until after the Crimean War.

After 1844 the Russian version of the spiked helmet, with a grenade finial instead of a spike, was issued to everyone who wore shakos, except for hussars. Cuirassiers received an intermediate pattern, those of the guards being surmounted by a three-dimensional double-headed eagle, in 1845, and the following year they were given all-metal helmets. Other forms of head-dress were the brass-fronted grenadier cap worn by other ranks of the Pavlovski Guard regiment (after 1825 this was also worn by the officers), the horse grenadier helmet with a transverse crest and a red cloth bag

hanging down the back, the square-topped *chapska* of the lancers, and the tapered so-called 'marine' shako.

The infantry, dragoons, and artillery retained their traditional dark green uniforms throughout the period, one of Nicholas's first acts being to make the jackets single-breasted, and to introduce trousers, green in winter and white in summer, in place of the former overalls, claiming to have made savings by both changes. Cuirassiers continued to wear white, lancers blue and hussars their usual wide range of colours.

From about 1829 the separate Caucasus corps began to evolve its own style of dress, the crack Nijegorodski dragoons adopting tall fur shakos, cossack blouses, baggy

A Regiment of Russian Grenadiers marching past, during the manoeuvres held at Vosnesensk, September 1837.

'The Brilliant Cavalry Action at Balaclava, 25 October 1854'. The heavy cavalry brigade, under the command of Major-General J. Y. Scarlett, here successfully charge and repulse the Russian cavalry prior to the more celebrated charge of the light brigade.

trousers, and Caucasian sabres hung from narrow shoulder belts. After 1848 tunics were in common wear in the Caucasus. During the Crimean War the Russian infantry usually fought in their greatcoats, with the skirts hooked up, and white trousers tucked into their boots. The spiked helmet seems to have been left behind with the baggage, in favour of a peakless forage cap in company colours, or a soft white linen peaked cap, another fashion imported from the Caucasus. The cavalry, at Balaclava at any rate, wore their full dress jackets under their thick sword-proof greatcoats.

The Prussian army was similar to the Russian in appearance, if not in its menacing might, harsh discipline and passion for uniformity. Family ties between the two countries were extremely close, and in 1835 guards units from both took part in joint manoeuvres in Prussian Poland. Prussia tried, unsuccessfully, to remain a great European power without incurring the expense of a large standing army. Conscription was kept low and the army seldom exceeded a strength of 200,000 men. Without conscription it was too small, and with conscription it became politically unreliable. Considered of no account by the country at large, it studiously modelled itself on its mighty neighbour Russia.

From 1816 to 1843 the infantry wore a variety of bell-topped shakos, generally smaller than the excessively tall Russian version. In 1824 metal fronted grenadier caps, said to have been a present from Alexander I, were issued to both battalions of the 1st Foot Guards. The uniforms were blue, except for *Jäger* and *Schützen* who wore grass green, guards regiments being distinguished by lace loops, *litzen*, on collars and cuffs. By 1836 grey trousers with red piping were in general wear, sometimes with brown marching gaiters. By 1817 the militia, or *Landwehr*, had been assimilated

FRANCE
Grenadier, 1853

Officer of the garde
mobile, 1870 (battalion
commander)

Zouave, 1859

Grenadier of the Imperial
Guard, 1870

Chasseur of the Imperial
Guard, 1857

FRANCE
Guards Carabinier
Regiment, 1869

Artillery Officer, 1849
(1854)

Dragoon, 1860

Guards Lancer, 1859

Cuirassier, 1870

FRANCE

Hussar of the 1st
Regiment of Hussars,
1853

Dragoon of the Dragoon
Guards Regiment, 1857

Uhlan, 1870

Chasseur d'Afrique, 1870

Chasseur à cheval, 1870

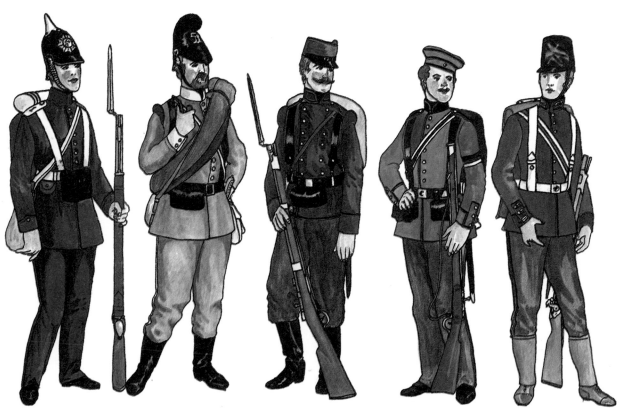

GERMAN STATES

Oldenburg, Infantryman,
1849

Bavaria, Infantryman of
the 8th Infantry Regiment,
1870

Württemburg, Infantryman
of the 7th Infantry
Regiment, 1870

Hessen-Kassel, Chasseur,
1866

Hanover, Infantryman,
1866

into the line organization, being chiefly distinguished by a blue edging to their collars, and the *Landwehr* cross, copied from the cross worn by the Russian militia, on their shakos.

Cuirassiers wore Russian-style leather helmets, white *Koller* and brass cuirasses, supposed to have been taken from the stores at Versailles in 1814, changed to steel in 1821. On special occasions the Garde du Corps wore the black cuirasses presented to them by Alexander I. Dragoons wore blue jackets and shakos, and lancers blue double-breasted jackets with striped girdles, and the traditional *chapska*. Guard cavalry, with the exception of hussars, were distinguished by collar and cuff *litzen*. Hussar uniforms went through several changes, particularly in 1836 when the jacket was lengthened and the braid loops given a different form. The *Landwehr* cavalry wore lancer dress but with shakos. In 1822 they were given the *chapska* with the cross in front. Guard *Landwehr* cavalry had *litzen* on collars and cuffs.

In 1843 the Prussian version of the spiked helmet, with a square metal-edged peak and a true spike, made its appearance. The guard retained their old eagle plate with the star of the order of the Black Eagle, while the line received a new pattern eagle. The *Jäger* at first received the helmet but changed, in 1854, to the low tapering shako, with front and back peaks, not unlike the Russian marine shako. The cuirassiers, dragoons and artillery also received the helmet, those of the former being made entirely of metal. The Garde du Corps and the Guard Cuirassier Regiment had a metal eagle, in place of the spike, for wear in full dress.

With the helmet came the tunic, so that from 1843 the Prussian army had already acquired the characteristic appearance which it kept until 1914. Soon after, new infantry equipment, with two waist pouches and braces, based on the French pattern, gave them an even more up-to-date appearance. The cavalry also received tunics, the *Koller* of the cuirassiers being laced around the collar and cuffs and down the fronts, and piped on the back seams and armholes. At the same time the Garde du Corps received *supervestes* for court duties, and in 1856 were given white breeches and jackboots. In 1855 the hussar tunic, known as the *attila* was introduced, and the pelisse abolished. Tall fur caps came in for some regiments and *mirlitons* for others. The lancers retained their jackets until after 1853, when the guard lancer regiment adopted the tunic, known in its lancer form as an *Ulanka*. In 1843 tunics and helmets, with the usual cross, were given to the *Landwehr*; and in 1852 the *Landwehr* cavalry were divided into types like the regular cavalry, whose uniforms they adopted apart from the cross on the head-dress.

The second most powerful of the 'reactionary' European powers, Austria, maintained a large army for policing her vast domains, in particular Italy. Being constantly employed the Austrian army suffered less than any other from the long period of peace after 1815, and was at the time considered to be the best in Europe. The troubles of 1848–9 in Austria, Hungary and Italy required the attention of so much of the army that Franz Joseph was forced to call upon Nicholas I for aid in 'pacifying' the Hungarians. The successful outcome of this campaign, and victory in Italy, strengthened Austria's position, but a vacillating policy during the Crimean War, and the loss of all her Italian provinces, except Venice, in 1859, led to a rapid decline in her military prowess.

Between 1816 and 1836 the Austrian infantry changed little in appearance. German regiments wore shakos, white coatees and breeches, and black gaiters; Hungarian regiments the same but with special cuffs and tight blue pantaloons; and the *Grenzer*, or frontier troops, the same as the Hungarians but with brown coatees. After 1830 grey trousers became the ordinary wear for German regiments. In 1836 the peak of the shako was straightened out to help the men in aiming, and the front plate of the fur grenadier caps was altered to a small grenade badge. At the same time light blue trousers were introduced for gala wear for officers of German regiments, and in 1851 Hungarian officers started wearing them as well as the undress grey trousers.

Between the same dates the German cavalry wore helmets, with woollen crests which were abolished in 1827, and white jackets, the cuirassiers having a patch of cloth of the facing colour on each side of the collar. In 1836 the hussar shako underwent the same straightening-out process as the infantry shako.

In 1849 the tunic was introduced together with a new system of rank stars on the collar. In the field, however, the infantry usually wore linen jackets with collar patches of the facing colour, and oilskin-covered shakos with white neck curtains. The dragoons received double-breasted white tunics, and the cuirassiers single-breasted with collar patches.

During the Hungarian rising of 1848–9 a national army, the *Honved*, was formed. The rebel regular Hungarian regiments wore their normal uniforms, with red, white and green Hungarian sashes and cockades, while the *Honved* troops wore shakos and tunics laced across in hussar fashion, and Hungarian pantaloons. The Hungarian revolution is remarkable for the eccentric costumes worn by the insurgents, of which the most celebrated was the befeathered broad-brimmed hat, later to become so popular with the Confederate

cavalry during the American Civil War.

An American observer, George B. McClellan, noted the excellence of the Austrian uniforms in 1855, remarking especially on the rifles in their blue-grey coats and hats, turned up at the sides and decorated with cock's feathers, the lancers in dark green tunics and *chapskas*, the hussars in light or dark blue tunics and shakos, and the heavy cavalry in their metal helmets.

After the restoration of the Bourbons in 1815 the French army went through a period when it was despised by all classes of society. By 1859, however, it was once again supreme in Europe. The turning point came in 1830 when France decided to settle her long-standing feud with the pirates who had been operating from Algiers for over 300 years. A force of 37,000 men was landed in North Africa in June, and on 5 July Algiers surrendered. After this *coup* the French army began speedily to pick up in quality and reputation. The civil disturbances which shook France in 1848 and brought Louis Napoleon to the fore, proved that the army could be useful in guarding lives and property, and won for it the grudging respect of the wealthy classes. In 1849 the army added to its new laurels by intervening successfully in Italy, where the Pope had been deposed by Garibaldi and Mazzini. In 1852 Louis Napoleon restored the hereditary monarchy, taking for himself the title of Napoleon III, and ruling from 1852–70 with a varying degree of autocracy at home, and professed liberalism abroad.

The French army emerged from the Crimean War with an enhanced reputation, and almost immediately embarked on a campaign to oust the Austrians from Italy, and to create an Italian state under Pope Pius IX. The notable French victories at Magenta and Solferino were attributed to the invincibility of her army, and between

PRUSSIA

Infantryman of the 21st Regiment of Foot, 1849

Officer of the 2nd Regiment of Foot Guards, 1870

Chasseur, 1866

Pioneer, 1864

Fusilier of the 33rd Fusilier Regiment, 1870

GERMAN STATES

Bavaria, Cuirassier, 1870

Baden, Dragoon, 1870

Hessen-Kassel, Hussar of the 2nd Hussar Regiment, 1866

Mecklenburg-Schwerin, Dragoon, 1866

Saxony, 1st Regiment of Heavy Cavalry, 1864

PRUSSIA

Drummer of the 2nd
Grenadier Guards
Regiment (Emperor
Francis'), 1860

Gunner of the Mounted
Artillery, 1870

Gunner of the Coastal
Artillery Section, 1870
(1877)

Hussar of the 3rd Reserve
Hussar Regiment, 1870

Trumpeter of the 9th
Dragoon Regiment, 1867

PRUSSIA

Dragoon of the 1st
Dragoon Regiment, 1866

Cavalry Headquarters
Company, 1870

Cuirassier of the 1st
Silesian Cuirassier
Regiment, 1870

Hussar of von Zieten's
Hussar Regiment, 1870

Uhlan of the 2nd
Brandenburg Uhlan
Regiment (11th), 1864

'The Italian camp at the Battle of Magenta, 4 June 1859' by Giovanni Fattori.

DENMARK

Guards Infantryman, 1864   Infantryman, 1848   Officer of the Leib Chasseurs, 1859   Infantryman, 1864   Dragoon, 1864

AUSTRIA

Infantryman of the 80th Infantry Regiment (Prince William of Glücksburg's), 1864   Officer of the Horse Artillery, 1866   Grenadier, 1850   Commander-in-Chief in greatcoat, 1855   Chasseur, 1859

AUSTRIA
Uhlan Officer, 1866
(temporary uniform)

Officer of the 8th Hussar
Regiment, 1859 (Elector
of Hessen's)

Dragoon, 1861

Uhlan, 1849

Officer of the 4th
Cuirassier Regiment

AUSTRIA
Drum-Major of the 18th
Infantry Regiment

Officer of the Krakow
Volunteers, 1866

Officer of the Styrian
Volunteer Rifles, 1848–50

Hungary, 1848, NCO,
Honved Infantry

Hungary, 1849, Uhlan of
Poninski's Uhlan Corps,
1848–9

'The Battle of Solferino,
1859'. This lithograph
shows the Piedmontese
attacking at San Martino.

1859 and 1870 countries as far apart as the United States of America, Turkey and Japan hired French advisers, and slavishly copied the new comfortable French styles. As it turned out, French fortunes declined dramatically after 1859. The Mexican fiasco of 1863–7, and the reputation of the Prussian army, which grew immensely after its defeat of the Austrians at Sadowa in 1866, led to a collapse in confidence in French imperialism. When war with Prussia came in 1870, the French army was as ready as ever to take part in the military enterprises of the era, but was not prepared for the fact that the era itself had changed.

As a result of campaign conditions in North Africa the French infantry abandoned their jackets and shakos, wearing their greatcoats alone, with a variety of peaked forage caps. These latter were regularized in 1833 as the *casquette*, a tall tapering cloth shako, which in due course became the celebrated *képi*. At the same time the infantry cross-belts were discarded in favour of black leather waist-belts, with a pouch in front and a bayonet frog at the side.

With the expansion of operations in North Africa new units were raised which were to gain world-wide renown, the *chasseurs d'Afrique*, the *zouaves* and the *spahis*. The dress of the first was romantic and practical at the same time, with a light blue tunic, brass epaulettes, voluminous red and blue sash, and baggy red trousers. The *spahis* were not given uniforms until 1841

The left-hand detail from 'The Capture of the Smala at Abd-el-Kadir, 1843' by Horace Vernet.

ITALY
Sardinia, Grenadier of the
Brigade of Guards
Grenadier Regiment, 1848

Sardinia, Grenadier of the
1st Grenadier Regiment,
1853

Modena, Infantryman,
1859

Officer of the Foot
Carabiniers, 1859

Bersagliere, 1866

ITALY
Sardinia, Dragoon of the
Nice Dragoon Regiment,
1844

Parma, Mounted Gunner
of the Field Artillery,
1853

Dragoon, 1866

Naples, Lancer, 1859

Naples, Dragoon of the 1st
Regiment, 1859

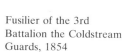

GREAT BRITAIN, Crimean War

Officer of the 77th
Regiment of Foot (East
Middlesex)

Infantryman of the 19th
Regiment, 1853

Fusilier of the 3rd
Battalion the Coldstream
Guards, 1854

Grenadier, 89th Regiment
of Foot, 1854

Officer of the 23rd or
Welsh Fusiliers, 1855

GREAT BRITAIN, Crimean War

Lancer of the 17th Lancers
Regiment, 1854

Hussar of the 8th Hussar
Regiment, 1854

Dragoon of the 2nd
Regiment of Dragoons
(North British
Dragoons–Scots Greys)

Officer of the Horse
Artillery, 1854

Dragoon of the 4th Light
Dragoon Regiment, 1854

when they were dressed in blue Arab waistcoats and trousers, red jackets and green burnouses. The *zouaves* at first wore a mixture of clothing, but by the time of the Crimean War their world-famous uniform had resolved itself into a red fez with a long tassel, wound round with a turban in full dress, blue jacket and waistcoat, baggy red trousers and yellow leather gaiters. McClellan described it as 'the most convenient dress possible'.

In 1839 a battalion of *chasseurs à pied* was formed at Vincennes, clothed in an experimental uniform based on African experience, and in the following year ten such battalions were assembled at St Omer under the Duc d'Orleans. The success of the experiment led to new dress regulations of 1845, which fixed the design of French uniforms for nearly thirty years.

The infantry wore a new shako, similar to that introduced for the *chasseurs d'Orleans*, which tapered towards the top, and sloped forward from the back, tunic, waist-belt equipment, and red trousers. The line infantry had blue collars, red cuffs, with a blue flap, and yellow buttons, and the light infantry yellow collars, blue pointed cuffs piped in yellow and white buttons. Officers had gold or silver epaulettes, gorgets, and waist-belts with two sword slings. The cavalry wore helmets and tunics, light blue for carabiniers, dark blue for cuirassiers, and green for dragoons. Lancers, who had been wearing the *kurtka* since 1837 were given *képis* with embroidered crossed lances in front. The *chasseurs à cheval* who also wore green underwent several changes, including, in 1839, a braided *dolman* which reached down to below the hips, and in 1848 a red shako. Hussars wore shakos, short braided dolmans, and strapped trousers, the colours of which varied from regiment to regiment.

In 1854 Napoleon III re-formed the *Garde Impériale*, dressed in a variety of uniforms which combined some features of the First Empire with heavy doses of the *style Rothschild* so beloved at the French court. The infantry consisting of grenadiers, *voltigeurs* and *chasseurs*, and the cavalry consisting of cuirassiers, lancers, dragoons, *chasseurs* and guides, created a kaleidoscopic effect as they paraded through the streets of Paris.

In 1861 a new and smaller shako was introduced, and the following year a double-breasted tunic. In 1868 dragoons and lancers were given tunics, and at the same time a trial hussar tunic was introduced but not actually adopted until 1872. The *garde nationale mobile*, a militia formed from those exempted from normal military service, wore the usual infantry uniform, but with blue-grey trousers. In 1868 various volunteer units, known as *franc-tireurs*, were raised and dressed in a variety of eccentric uniforms, including wide-brimmed hats and feathers, grey, brown or blue blouses, baggy trousers and *zouave* gaiters. During the Franco-Prussian war the Germans refused to recognize them as regular units and shot them when they were taken prisoner. Later on, in order to prevent this happening, they were dressed as far as possible like the *garde mobile*.

One of the armies most influenced by France was that of Sardinia, whose ruler Victor Emmanuel became the first king of a unified Italy. The infantry, in their shakos or blue *képis*, blue tunics and light blue-grey trousers, looked to McClellan strikingly like his own Americans. The famous *Bersaglieri*, raised in 1833 by General Lamarmora as an embodiment of the best features of the light infantry of the time, wore blue tunics and *zouave* trousers, and distinctive broad-brimmed hats with a plume of cocks' feathers. The cavalry wore dark blue tunics, blue-grey breeches, and a

low French shako usually in a yellow oilskin cover. McClellan thought that the appearance of the Sardinian army in the Crimea was superior to that of either of its allies.

Perhaps the most unlikely disciples of the French were the Russians, the period after the Crimean War marking the beginning of the close relationship between the two countries that was to last until 1914. Soon after the peace was signed Alexander II paid a state visit to Napoleon III, who hoped to find, in Russia, an ally in the coming struggle against Prussia. With her western flank secured to some extent by the subsequent French alliance, Russia was free to continue her expansionist policy in the south and east undisturbed. In 1864 the Caucasus was finally conquered and Russia turned her attention to Central Asia. Widespread reforms, brought about by the humiliation suffered by Russia during and immediately after the Crimean War, affected both civilian and military life. The reform and modernization of the army and

its weapons was accompanied by the introduction of the new loose style of clothing, the very antithesis of the spirit of Nicholas I.

The short jacket had already been abolished for all arms during the Crimean War, and the tunic, or *demi-kaftan*, took its place. The spiked helmet was also done away with, except for generals and the Preobrajenski guard regiment, in favour of the tapering marine shako. The old helmet plate was changed to one with a double-headed eagle with upright wings in the Austrian style. In 1862 the French shako, together with the *képi* for undress, was introduced for all arms except cuirassiers and lancers. The cuffs, collars and other details of the tunic remained the same as they had been under Nicholas I, but the cut was made slightly looser. Another important development was the introduction of gold- or silver-laced 'shoulder-boards' for officers which gradually took the place of epaulettes, except for dress occasions. They originated in the custom of Russian officers,

'The Battle of Inkerman'. The British Foot Guards hold off the massed Russians appearing on the heights, while the French General Bosquets' division hurries to their relief.

A detail from Simeon Fort's watercolour of the night attack on Constantine by way of the bridge of El Cantara on 23 November 1836.

who had no greatcoats of their own, only cloaks or *surtouts*, wearing soldiers' coats on campaign, some say during the Russo-Turkish War of 1828–30, and others during the Crimean War. On to the soldiers' coloured shoulder-straps they had sewn strips of lace, field officers having one broad and two narrow leaving two stripes of the backing colour, and subalterns two broad leaving one stripe down the middle.

We have now reached what is virtually the half-way mark in the story of military

costume between 1815 and 1914. By 1870 the armies of Europe had almost without exception modified their previously impractical full dress into a practical dress, inspired chiefly by the example of the French. Then came the Franco-Prussian War and the emergence in 1871 of the German Empire of over 40 million people, which rapidly upset the balance of power and led to a period of militarism and re-armament culminating in the holocaust of 1914.

The American Civil War
and After
1860-1914

7

JOHN MOLLO

Of the countries that were most influenced by French fashions, the United States of America had, until 1850, been chiefly influenced by the British, but in 1851 the French tunic and *casquette* were introduced for the whole army. The latter came with a coloured pom-pom, eagle cap plate, and in the cavalry, thick braided 'flounders'. The dragoons had orange-yellow 'arm of service' distinctions, the mounted rifles green, the artillery red, and the infantry 'Saxony' blue. The infantry were given black leather equipment consisting of a waist-belt, from which hung the bayonet, and a cross-belt with a cartouche box. At the same time they were issued with the blue 'four button blouse' and *képi* which were to become the celebrated dress of the Civil War period.

In 1854 the shell jacket was restored to the cavalry, and in the following year the newly raised 1st and 2nd Cavalry appeared in the felt hats named alternatively after Major Hardee of the 2nd Cavalry, or Jeff Davis, the Secretary of War. In 1861 the government placed an order in France for 10,000 complete equipments 'to be uniformed as Chasseurs à Pied'. Thus the whole of the United States infantry was very nearly clothed in this fashion.

On the outbreak of the Civil War in 1861 it was the state volunteers and militia who came to the aid of the hard-pressed North. In the years before the war these units had far from stinted themselves in the matter of dress. There were highlanders in feathered bonnets, 'Highland Fusiliers' in tartan trews, grenadiers in red tunics and bearskin caps, 'German Artillery' in spiked helmets, lancers in *chapskas*, the New York Garibaldi Guards in *zouave* trousers, red shirts, and *Bersaglieri* hats adorned with cocks' feathers. The New York Fire Zouaves were typical of several units on both sides which, in the early years of the

war, went into action in full Arab costume.

Contrary to popular belief the Northern troops during the Civil War were not clothed exclusively in blue, nor the Southerners in grey. The dress regulations for the army of Georgia, published in 1861, specify a blue flannel 'sack' for fatigue dress and a black felt hat, although officers could wear the *képi*. The enlisted men of North Carolina were to have a 'sack coat' and trousers of North Carolina grey and felt hats, the officers again being permitted to wear 'French forage caps' off-duty. The Confederate cavalry affected a very dashing appearance, reminiscent of Garibaldi and Kossuth, with feathered hats, short grey jackets with yellow lapels buttoned back, and French rank braiding on their sleeves.

After a few months of campaigning, however, the glitter of the elaborate uniforms worn by both sides was sadly dimmed. Materials were often shoddy and the workmanship of the trimmings tawdry, and before long faded blue coats and trousers, or suits of home-dyed 'butternut', became the common fighting wear. Gradually items of regulation uniform and equipment were modified or abandoned. For instance, the white linen *képi* covers and neck curtains, known as 'Havelocks' after the British General of Indian Mutiny fame, and issued to both sides at the beginning of the war, were soon relegated to the role of dish-cloths or coffee-strainers. The stiff felt 'Jeff Davis' hat, worn turned up on the right side by officers and the cavalry and on the left by the infantry, and even the *képi* itself were frequently abandoned in favour of a good soft felt hat, while the elegant pale blue caped greatcoat was condemned as 'a great inconvenience' on service. Broad flat-heeled shoes, when available, were found preferable to boots, and spats or leggings, when issued, were soon discarded or gave way to stockings rolled up over the

'The Battle of Gettysburg – Charge of the Confederates on Cemetery Hill, Thursday night, 2 July 1863'. The Confederate assault ran out of thrust as the men stormed strong Federal positions on the appropriately named Cemetery Hill.

The Confederate asssault
on Fort Saunders on
29 November 1863. The
Confederates were led by
General Longstreet and the
Union troops by General
Burnside.

The German artillery in
action at Gravelotte, August
1870, during the
Franco-Prussian War,
1870–1.

trouser legs. The heavy knapsack, which if not carefully packed, bore uncomfortably on the wearer's back, was given up for a single blanket roll, worn over the shoulder, with the spare clothes, if any, wrapped inside. It was found 'inconvenient to change the underwear too often . . . the better way was to dress out and out, and wear that outfit until the enemy's knapsacks, or the folks at home supplied a change'. The tin or wooden canteen was also dropped in favour of a large tin cup which could double as a drinking vessel and as a saucepan for boiling coffee. This wholesale jettisoning of unwanted equipment was often carried to excessive lengths bordering on the foolhardy.

The cavalry gradually abandoned their stiff hats and brass shoulder-scales, and adopted the practice of fastening their sabres to the near fore-part of the saddle, with the hilt facing forward so that it could be easily seized by the right hand. The officers gradually adopted the four button blouse in place of the long frock coat, and by the end of the war the crimson officers' sash had virtually disappeared.

The Northern soldier on the whole went to war as sensibly equipped as any of that era, and shortages of clothing and equipment tended to be temporary. On the other hand the acute lack of necessaries in the Southern army was chronic. Nevertheless, 'between the spinning wheels of his womenfolk and the plunder from the abundantly stocked Yankee supply depots, Johnny Reb managed to keep going, and any deficiency in his wardrobe was not reflected in his fighting ability'. After the war the regular army continued to wear their pre-war uniforms without change until 1872.

By 1867 the insignificant Prussian army of 1859 had become the victorious army soon to be reinforced by the armies of the North German Federation. By 1870 Prussia had some 1,180,000 men at her disposal, and with the formation of the Imperial army in 1871 the whole of the land forces of the German Federation came under the direct control of the Emperor.

The 'handsome and practical' uniform of the German army remained basically unchanged from 1870 to 1914. The infantry wore the spiked helmet and blue tunic, with grey-black trousers for ordinary duties and white duck for parades, when horsehair plumes were worn in place of the spike. The helmet went through numerous modifications ending up, around 1900, lower and rounder with curved front and back peaks. Changes in cut resulted in shorter skirts, and the campaigns of 1864, 1866, and 1870 established the custom of wearing the trousers tucked into the boots on active service. *Jäger* and *Schützen* continued to wear the low shako with front and back peaks, and grass green tunics.

Changes in cavalry uniforms were even more minute. Cuirassiers retained their metal helmets and white *Koller*, but after 1889 cuirasses were no longer worn in the field. Instead officers of all regiments, other ranks of the two guards regiments, and NCOs of line regiments wore the dark blue single-breasted *Waffenrock*. Dragoons kept their spiked helmets and cornflower-blue tunics, and lancers their *chapskas* and dark blue *ulankas*. The various hussar regiments were distinguished by the colour of the cloth bags of their low fur caps, and by the colour of their *attilas*. The Prussian hussars retained the traditional hussar items of barrel sash and sabretache. All guards regiments, with the exception of the hussars, had gold or silver, or in the case of the men yellow or white *litzen* on collars and cuffs.

The other states that made up the German Empire retained many of their distinctive uniform features. The Saxons, in particular, kept their light blue cavalry and

TURKEY

Artilleryman, 1855   Infantryman, 1855   Cavalryman, 1855   Artillery Officer, 1855   Cavalryman, 1877–8

RUSSIA

Staff officer of an Infantry
Regiment of the indepen-
dent Caucasian Corps, 1855   Infantryman, 1849   Grenadier, 1854   Infantryman, 1877–8   Sergeant of a Caucasian
Rifle Battalion, 1854

RUSSIA

NCO of the Empress'
Mounted Guards, 1850

Dragoon of the Leibgarde,
1850

Hussar, 1850

Tsarevich's Guards Uhlan
Regiment, 1850

Grenadier of the Mounted
Grenadier Guards, 1850

RUSSIA

Guards Gendarmerie,
1852

Artillery Officer, 1877–8

Grenadier of the
Leibgarde Grenadier
Regiment, 1855

Grenadier Guardsman,
Palace Guard, 1855

Artilleryman of the
Caucasian Cossacks, 1840

The German Infantry and *Jäger* in defensive positions along the railway line at Bethincourt in the Franco-Prussian War.

dark green artillery tunics, while in Bavaria the predominant colour of the infantry was light blue, and the cavalry light blue and green. The German units were renumbered consecutively with the Prussian army, and the whole wore two cockades on their head-dress, one red, white and black for the German Empire and the other in the state colours.

After 1880 Germany set about acquiring an overseas empire, and from the police and *Schütztruppen*, raised to guard her new possessions in Africa and the Far East, came

the grey uniform, with coloured piping, riding breeches and boots so typical of German uniforms from 1914 to 1945. In 1898 troops on manoeuvres appeared in full dress, but with grey helmet covers, and three years later an experimental grey uniform consisting of felt spiked helmet, fly-fronted *bluse*, trousers, brown boots and equipment, was tried out in the Far East. In the same year special machine-gun detachments were formed, dressed in a grey-green uniform, and in February 1910, after various other trials, the *feldgrau* service dress, in which the German front line troops went to war in 1914, was introduced.

After her defeats at the hands of the French and Sardinians in 1859 and the Prussians in 1866, culminating in her expulsion from the German Federation, Austria was forced to come to terms with her Hungarian subjects. In 1867 Franz-Joseph was crowned King of Hungary, and the dual monarchy of Austria-Hungary was thus formed. In 1877 Austria, prompted by Germany, stayed out of the Russo-Turkish War, and in return was awarded administrative rights over the Balkan provinces of Bosnia and Hertzegovina. In 1908 and 1909 when these became critical areas, the Austrian connection enabled Germany to intervene in Balkan affairs, thus setting a precedent which was to have calamitous results in 1914.

Between 1859 and 1870 the Austrian army altered little in appearance. In 1861 a new tunic was introduced, with shorter rounder skirts, and a turned down collar. On service, however, the infantry usually wore greatcoats only, like the French, but with the skirts hooked up on the inside. The cuirass was abolished in 1860, and in 1868 the cuirassiers themselves were amalgamated with the dragoons.

Perhaps the most significant development sartorially speaking was the formation of a number of regiments of Hungarian volunteers for service in Italy. These carried on the romantic traditions of the *Honved* of 1848–9, wearing a variety of costumes based partly on Hungarian folk dress. Their importance is that from all the mass of fur, feathers, pelisses, knickerbockers and high boots emerged, as early as 1866, the prototype of the modern service dress jacket with flapped pockets on breast and hips.

The rationalization of the dress of the Austrian army after 1870 served, with little alteration, as a full dress until 1914. The infantry abandoned their time-honoured white uniforms, which were henceforth worn by general officers only, for a simple dark blue tunic with regimental collar and cuffs and a black shako. German regiments wore blue-grey trousers, and Hungarians their special cuffs and tight pantaloons. Officers had gold lace round their shakos, yellow waist sashes, and piping down the front of their tunics. The *Tyroler-Kaiser-Jäger* and the independent rifle battalions wore hats with turned up brims and cocks' feathers, and grey uniforms with green facings.

By 1882 an undress uniform was coming into general use. For officers it consisted of a black *képi* and a dark blue *bluse*, with four outside pockets and collar patches of the regimental colour on which the rank stars were set. The rank and file had a similar *bluse* with a cloth roll, or pad, on the right shoulder to prevent the rifle slipping off. Their head-dress consisted of a light blue *Feldkappe*, with a black leather peak, yellow metal cockade, and two ear-flaps which folded up and buttoned in front. The *bluse* of the *Jäger* and rifles was *hechtgrau*, or light grey. The *Landwehr* infantry wore light grey blouses with green shoulder-straps and collar-patches, blue-grey trousers with a green stripe and a blue-grey *Feldkappe*. The Hungarian *Honved* infantry wore dark blue frocks with red braiding on collar and cuffs, light blue pantaloons piped in red, and the normal infantry field cap.

Dragoons wore black leather helmets with front and back peaks, gilt or brass ornaments and a plate with the double-headed eagle and the Imperial arms. The field cap was made entirely of madder-red cloth, including the peak. The single-breasted tunic had regimental collar and cuffs, and the pelisse, or *pelzrock*, was light blue with a black astrakhan collar. Unlike

RUSSIA

Dragoon, 1897   Infantryman, 1905   General, 1905   Cossack of the 3rd   Artillery officer, 1905
Regiment of Orenburg
Cossacks, 1905

JAPAN

Guards Infantry, 1905   Infantryman, 1905   Officer, 1905   General, 1905   Cavalryman, 1905

SPAIN
Cuban Volunteer   Infantry, 1900   Artillery, 1900   Cuban Volunteer   Cavalry of the Cuban
Battalion, 1898   Battalion, 1898   Volunteers, 1898

USA
General, 1901   Trooper of the 1st   Infantryman, 1898   Infantryman, 1898   Officer in China,
                      Volunteer Cavalry   1901
                      Regiment, 1898

the hussar pelisse it was made large enough to be worn over the tunic. Madder-red breeches and black boots, with straight tops, completed the uniform.

Hussars wore a shako of regimental colour with a straight black horsehair plume, and a madder-red field cap. The *attila* was light or dark blue, trimmed with black and yellow cord, and the pelisse was lined with black astrakhan. The tight madder-red pantaloons were worn with Hessian boots. Lancers wore the *chapska* with the upper part in the regimental colour, and a drooping black horsehair plume. Their field cap was madder red. The *Ulanka* was light blue and had three outside pockets and madder-red collar and cuffs. Light blue *pelzrock*, madder-red breeches and dragoon boots completed their uniform. The *Landwehr* cavalry were clothed as lancers or dragoons, and the *Honved* cavalry like hussars, with shakos of regimental colour, madder red field caps, dark blue frocks faced and trimmed in red, dark blue pelisses with red trimming and white fur, madder-red pantaloons with red trimming and hussar boots.

The Austrian army, which could with justification take the credit for the invention of service dress, with the *bluse* and *Feldkappe*, was slow to follow this development to its logical conclusion. By 1890 the field cap was worn by everyone except the cavalry and artillery, but it was not until 1909 that a light grey service dress made its appearance. First issued to the infantry and *Landwehr* only, it consisted of a blouse, trousers and greatcoat all made of the same light grey material. The men kept the old light blue field cap, and the officers were given a similar one to take the place of the dark blue *képi*. It was in this uniform that the Austrian infantry entered the First World War.

Having examined the uniforms of the two 'Central Powers' up to 1914, we must now turn our attention to three of their opponents, the United States of America, France, and Russia. After the Civil War the United States army was used mainly to protect the western frontier, and for occasional police duties. It was therefore much reduced and by 1890 was only some 25,000 men strong. The cavalry, however, vitally needed in the Indian fighting on the frontier, was kept up to a strength of ten regiments. In the late 1890s the United States became embroiled with Spain over the question of conditions in Cuba, and in the 'splendid little war' which followed the former acquired not only Cuba but Puerto Rico and the Philippines as well, thus suddenly joining the ranks of the colonial powers. In 1900, during the Boxer rising, an American force was sent to assist in the relief of the legations at Peking, and from then on American influence spread throughout the world, particularly in Latin America and the Far East.

In 1872 the army was given a new uniform, the biggest innovation of which was the black felt spiked helmet, of German inspiration, for the mounted branches. This had gold cap-lines and flounders for the officers, front and back peaks edged with leather, an eagle plate and a horsehair plume. The plumes and cap-lines of the rank and file were in the branch colour, yellow for cavalry, red for artillery, and orange for signal troops. The uniform itself consisted of a dark blue single-breasted tunic and blue-grey trousers. Collar and cuff patches, piping and trouser stripes were in the branch colour. Officers had double-breasted tunics and gold epaulettes of enormous size and ugliness. The rank and file also had an undress of a dark blue *képi*, and after 1874 a dark blue 'five button blouse' with collar and cuffs edged with braid of the branch colour.

The cavalry field-dress, in which Colonel Custer's celebrated 7th Cavalry rode to their deaths at the Little Big Horn, consisted of a black slouch hat, the five button blouse or a plain blue shirt, black leather boots worn over canvas reinforced breeches and gauntlet gloves. The officers wore double-breasted shirts sometimes trimmed with white or yellow braid. The hat went through a variety of changes. The 'Hardee' hat had proved oppressive in hot weather, so the authorities resurrected the 'Andrews' hat which had been issued to some of the cavalry in 1851. This was made of pearl-grey or stone-coloured felt and had a very wide brim which could be 'cocked' like an eighteenth-century hat. This in turn inspired the 'campaign hat' of 1872, which being made of black 'velvet-finished' felt soon proved wanting under active service conditions. After several attempts to improve it, it was finally replaced by the more solid drab 'bush hat' of Boy Scout shape.

In 1872 the infantry received a new shako, based on the French model, but in 1881 this was changed for a modified version of the helmet. The tunics were similar to those of the cavalry, but with bright blue trimming. When the helmet was introduced it came with a white plume, so in 1884 the infantry colour was correspondingly changed to white. The valise and pouch equipment, introduced in 1872, was soon discarded in action, the American soldier preferring to carry his kit in a blanket roll over his shoulder, and his ammunition in a cartridge belt.

Between 1880 and 1898 there were minor changes in US uniforms. In 1881 cork, or 'paper', helmets covered in white drill were introduced for summer wear. In 1892 officers, who until then had been wearing a version of the five button blouse, with the old Civil War rank badges on the shoulders, were given an elaborately frogged 'patrol' jacket, similar to that worn in the British army. In 1895 this was replaced by a buttonless dark blue 'sack coat' edged all round with dark blue mohair braid. At the same time they were given a new forage cap, with a stiff crown and a straight up-and-down peak.

When the Cuban War broke out a khaki tropical service dress had already been introduced, but few of the troops taking part were issued with it. Instead they wore a variant of the field uniform in use in the 1880s, consisting of the drab campaign hat, blue shirt, blue-grey trousers and brown canvas leggings. The infantry equipment consisted of a blanket and belongings wrapped up in a 'shelter-half', slung over the shoulder, and a webbing cartridge belt, from which hung the haversack and bayonet. The hurriedly raised volunteer units wore an assortment of clothing; the famous 1st US Volunteer Cavalry, Theodore Roosevelt's 'Roughriders', embarked on the war in campaign hats, brown canvas stable blouses and trousers and brown leggings.

With the stationing of considerable garrisons in the Far East khaki came more and more into use. Then, in 1902, the universal 'olive-drab' service dress made its appearance. This consisted of the drab campaign hat, an olive-green tunic with a high closed collar bearing bronze branch badges, breeches, brown leather boots for the officers and canvas leggings for the men. In 1903 a new pattern of webbing equipment was introduced. This had nine separate covered pouches on the belt, which was pierced with a series of holes from which hung the haversack, bayonet and entrenching tool, the remaining kit being carried, as before, across the body in a blanket roll. In 1910, however, a revolutionary system of equipment appeared in which the blanket

USA
Indiana Volunteers
(Wallace's Zouaves),
1860–4

Trooper, 1860–4

Infantry Officer, 1860–4

Infantryman, 1860–4

Sergeant of the Light
Artillery

USA
Infantryman in marching
uniform, 1860–4

Trooper in cloak, 1860–4

Lieutenant-General,
1860–4

Major-General, 1860–4

Artillery Officer, 1860–4

CONFEDERATE STATES, 1860–4

Trooper, 1860–4   Infantryman, 1860–4   Artillery Officer, 1860–4   Cavalry Officer,   Infantry Officer, 1860–4
                                                                                    1860–4

CONFEDERATE STATES, 1860–4

Trooper, 1860–4   General (Cavalry), 1860–4   General (Infantry), 1860–4   Gunner of the Mounted   Infantryman, 1860–4
                                                                                              Artillery, 1860–4

'The storming of the farm at Sevigny by the 11th Regiment of Chasseurs in 1870' by W. Beauquesne.

roll, haversack, bayonet and entrenching tool were all attached to a 'pack carrier', which was carried on the back in Indian, or 'papoose' fashion. This basic idea, although subsequently modified, survived until 1956.

After 1871 France was obsessed with the idea of obtaining vengeance for the humiliations she had received at the hands of Germany, and by 1890, after a series of successful colonial campaigns in Algeria and elsewhere, the morale of the army was in great measure restored. The secret military treaty with Russia, the *Entente Cordiale* with Britain, dating from 1904, and German interference in the Balkans all helped to strengthen the alliance against the 'central powers', Germany and Austria. Under the Third Republic both the Imperial Guard and the *Garde Nationale Mobile* were disbanded, otherwise the army remained basically the same as it had

been under the Second Empire.

In matters of dress the chief alteration, apart from the removal of various Imperial emblems, was in the lowering of the shako and *képi* peaks from the horizontal to an angle of about thirty degrees. The 1872 uniforms of the rank and file of the infantry were much as they had been in 1867. The officers wore a tunic similar to that of the men, until 1884 when it was replaced by the dark blue *dolman*, or patrol jacket, with seven brandenbourgs of black braid across the chest. In the following year their shakos were abolished so that in full dress they differed entirely from their men. This situation was however gradually rectified. From 1886 a stiffened red *képi* replaced the shako for the men, and in 1893 a short loose tunic, single-breasted and with red collar and cuff patches, was ordered for the officers. Finally in 1899 the single-breasted tunic was given to the men, so that once again they were dressed alike. The epaulettes, which had been discontinued during the *dolman* period, were restored for full dress. The *Chasseurs à pied* went through similar changes, but retained their distinctive colours and white metal buttons. The infantry trousers remained madder-red throughout the period, and by 1880 the cloaks and greatcoats for the whole army were blue-grey.

The cavalry also went through similar changes. In cuirassier regiments the officers were permitted to wear the *dolman*, while in the dragoons for a time all ranks wore them. In 1882 the heavy cavalry were still wearing tunics with long skirts, which were turned back when mounted to show the red lining. A year or so later they were replaced with new tunics with short skirts. All light cavalry wore a light blue *dolman* with nine cord brandenbourgs across the chest. *Chasseurs à cheval* had light blue shakos with a bugle badge, and hussars the same but with an Austrian knot in cord in front. In 1881 a trial helmet was issued to the 11th *Chasseurs*. It was not unlike the American helmet, but was covered in light blue cloth and had black leather front and back peaks, and a curb chain chin-strap passing diagonally across the front, which bore a small tricolour cockade and a bugle for *chasseurs*, and an Austrian knot for hussars.

In the 1890s 'knicker' breeches, riding breeches which widened out extravagantly above the knee became fashionable for officers. By 1897 the *Chasseurs alpins* were appearing in large blue berets, blue tunics with turned down collars, blue-grey knickerbockers, and blue *puttees*, copied from the British. But in spite of numerous attempts France was singularly unsuccessful in developing a practical service dress. In the colonies white helmets with khaki covers, white or khaki clothing, and black or khaki *puttees* were worn by European troops, but in metropolitan France nothing could seemingly shake the supremacy of the red *képi* and trousers.

In 1903 an experimental blue-grey uniform was tried out, consisting for officers a slouch hat turned up on the right side, a pocketless tunic and trousers. There was a simplified system of rank markings on the sleeves, and epaulettes were to be worn in full dress. The men had the slouch hat, a loose *vareuse* with a wide turned down collar, trousers and leather anklets. The opinion of the army and the public was very much against this uniform and it was soon abandoned. Next came a proposal to replace the *képi* with a 'light helmet or casque of aluminium', which also failed to find favour. In 1911 yet another projected uniform appeared with a low khaki-covered helmet, piped in red, blue scarf, khaki *vareuse*, trousers and *puttees*; and two years later the celebrated battle-painter Detaille came up with a new helmet reminiscent of a seventeenth-century pikeman's combe-helmet. None of these experiments was acceptable and in 1914 the French army went to war in full dress, the infantry with blue covers over their *képis*, and the cuirassiers and dragoons with their glittering helmets in khaki covers.

The spirit of reform did not survive long in Russia, and by 1870 increasing revolutionary activity had generated a 'backlash' against the liberalism of Alexander II. In 1881 he was assassinated by those he was trying to help, and was succeeded by his son Alexander III, a reactionary whose policy of 'Russifying' all aspects of life turned half the Russian Empire into potential enemies, to the further advantage of the revolutionary 'activists'. Russian intervention against the Turks, in the fight for Balkan freedom, only served to worsen relations with Britain,

Scouts of the 10th Bengal Lancers in Field Service order in the 1890s, by R. Simkin.

Germany and Austria, and as a result greater reliance was placed on the alliance with France, who continued to pour money into Russia in a massive modernization campaign. Much of this was spent on re-equipping the army which was now a modern fighting force compared with that which had fought in the Crimea, although as such it was still riddled with inefficiency. In matters of dress, however, what foreign influence there was tended to be from Britain or Germany rather than from France.

There was little change in the basic Russian uniform during the last part of the reign of Alexander II, apart from the introduction of a new sash for officers, without tassels, and fastening in front with a *pass* like the lancer girdle. Progress was, however, made with the development of a service dress with the wearing, in Central Asia, of the native Russian shirt, with its stand collar and side opening, belted around the

The 20th Bengal (Punjab) Native Infantry in field service order escorting a baggage train on the march, by R. Simkin.

waist outside the trousers. The addition of the coloured shoulder-straps from the tunic gave the *gymnasterka*, as it was called, a jaunty military air. *Képis* were worn with white covers and neck curtains, and in Turkestan rawhide trousers, dyed red, proved efficacious against scorpion bites. During the Russo-Turkish War of 1877–8 the Russian troops wore their normal uniforms, with greatcoats in winter, and white *gymnasterka*, or tunics for the officers, in summer. The all-white linen peaked cap, formerly worn in the Caucasus and the Crimea, still remained extremely popular.

Alexander III abolished the buttoned tunic in November 1881, and for reasons of economy, tinged with parsimony, introduced a new uniform throughout the army. The whole of the line cavalry were converted to dragoons and were given, as head-dress, the *dragoonka*, a small round fur cap with a stiff crown in the regimental facing colour. With it came a dark green double-breasted tunic, or *kaftan*, fastening in front with hooks, blue-grey breeches and soft boots. The tunic was made very loose with gathers at the waist and pockets on each side for carrying extra cartridges. In undress officers and senior NCOs wore peaked, and the rank and file peakless forage caps. The *shashka*, or sabre, worn in the Caucasian manner suspended from a narrow shoulder belt, was introduced in various forms for most of the army.

The infantry had a similar uniform but with a small fur pillbox cap, and baggy dark green trousers tucked inside the boots. The guard infantry and dragoons were given the new uniform, with *litzen* on collars and cuffs, and the star of the order of St Andrew on their cap-badges. The Pavlovski Regiment, however, kept their mitre caps, and the remainder of the guard cavalry and the cossacks, their old uniforms.

The new uniform, which was still in use when Nicholas II came to the throne in 1894, was worn during the Russo-Japanese War of 1904–5, the only concession to winter active service being the issue of large shaggy fur caps to the troops at the front. The humiliating defeat suffered by Russia in this war shattered the morale of the army for some time, and in 1908 certain changes were made in an attempt to restore it. Buttons were added to the *kaftans* of the cavalry first and then of the infantry, and the unpopular fur caps were abolished and replaced by forage caps, for a short time embellished with the full dress cap badge. The dragoons were given back their former titles and uniforms, except for the cuirassiers who nevertheless received their old uniform back again. In 1909, in a last burst of romantic militarism, the guards regiments were given back their distinctive *plastrons* and a modernized version of the 1812 *kiwer*, smaller in size and made of coloured cloth, with a black leather top.

In 1908 a khaki service dress was introduced, consisting of a peaked cap bearing the oval Russian cockade, and a jacket, or *kittel*, with pockets for the officers and without for the men. Two years later the other ranks' *kittel* was replaced by the khaki *gymnasterka*. The infantry wore khaki trousers tucked into marching boots, and the cavalry and horse artillery their normal, mostly blue-grey, breeches and boots. At first officers wore their gold- or silver-laced shoulder-boards in service dress, but before long a special khaki version of the lace was introduced. The rank and file wore reversible cloth shoulder-straps, khaki on one side, and coloured as for full dress on the other. In 1912 a British-style Sam Browne belt, with two cross braces, was introduced for officers.

In 1913 the Romanov dynasty celebrated its tercentenary, and the khaki uniform was adapted to make it more suitable for wear at the ceremonies which took place all over Russia. A false *plastron*, with buttons and collar attached, was added to the *kittel* and *gymnasterka*, but this absurd idea was soon found to be impracticable. The tall tapering fur cap, with ear-flaps, also issued on this occasion was, however, retained for winter service dress, and was worn right through the First World War and the ensuing revolution.

Thus the golden century of military uniform, during which fashion after fashion had been introduced and discarded according to the tastes of autocrats, the romantic aspirations of revolutionaries, the economics of growing industry, as well as the hard facts of campaign life, had come to an end. Almost everywhere modern service dress in khaki or grey had prevailed over the colourful uniforms of the past.

The First World War and the Restless Peace 1914-39

8

GUIDO ROSIGNOLI

GERMANY

Bavaria, Leib Infantry Regiment in field service uniform, 1914

Prussia, 16th Infantry Regiment (3rd Westphalian, Freiherr von Sparr's)

Hessen-Darmstadt, 117th Infantry Leib Regiment (3rd Hessian, Grand Duchess'), 1918

Uhlan of the 11th Uhlan Regiment (2nd Brandenburg, Count Haeseler's)

Hussar of the 8th Hussar Regiment (1st Westphalian)

EASTERN EUROPE

Bulgaria, Infantry Officer, 1914

Turkey, Cavalryman, 1915

Turkey, Infantry Officer, 1915

Turkey, Infantryman, 1915

Bulgaria, Infantryman, 1915

AUSTRIA

Private of the 14th Infantry
Regiment, 1914

Dragoon of the 3rd
Dragoon Regiment, 1914

Private of the 84th Infantry
Regiment, 1918

Hussar, 1914

Officer of the Imperial
Tyrolean Chasseurs, 1914

Greece, Infantryman, 1916

Montenegro, NCO of a
machine-gun section, 1914

Czech Legion in the
Russian service, 1914

Serbia, Infantryman, 1914

Portugal, Infantryman,
1917–18

During the early years of the twentieth century the growing political instability in Europe made the possibility of a large-scale international conflict increasingly evident. In the face of these developments the general staffs of the major European armies began to make preparations for war. In the field of uniform the advantages of the khaki battledress, which had been gradually adopted by troops serving in the European colonial empires, were obvious, although the old blue and red uniforms continued to be used for some time by units serving at home. Moreover, apart from the practical advantages of the khaki dress, the adoption of a plain dull-coloured combat uniform became imperative because of the expense of equipping large armies with the old coloured uniforms.

The major powers approached this problem from different points of view. The British army had invented 'khaki' half a century earlier, had tested a number of uniforms in colonial warfare and therefore opted for khaki field uniforms which began to be issued in 1902. The officers wore the peaked cap, tunic, breeches, riding boots or boots with leggings. The original Sam Browne belt had two braces crossed at the back which held an ammunition pouch, the revolver holster and the sword. Later, one shoulder brace only was used and the sword was also eliminated. A jacket with open collar, showing the shirt and tie, and with four very large patch pockets replaced the tunic in about 1914 and, bar minor modifications, is still in use nowadays.

The first khaki other ranks' head-dress was the Broderick cap, which resembled the sailors' hat, but was soon replaced by a normal peaked cap with the typical British cloth-covered visor. Later, during the war, a peaked cap with folded ear flaps was issued, and another one with the cloth visor stiffened by lines of stitches. Steel helmets appeared eventually but did not become available to everyone until 1917. The soldiers' tunic was single-breasted with stand-and-fall collar, shoulder straps and four pockets with flaps, the breast ones with pleats. Additional strengthening patches were sewn at the front, below the shoulder straps. The soldiers on foot had trousers and puttees and were issued in 1908 with the webbing equipment that remained in use until the late 1930s. Mounted troops wore leggings and were issued with different field equipment. The Scots wore a Balmoral-type bonnet, tunics with rounded front skirts and a khaki apron which covered the front and back of the kilt.

A similar uniform, but made of light khaki drill cloth, was used in hot climates, usually accompanied by the Wolseley pattern cork helmet; shorts could be worn instead of trousers. Commonwealth troops wore khaki uniforms similar to the British pattern, although often pocket flaps and other tunic details were different, combined with distinguishing national head-dresses, for instance the wide-brimmed hats of the Anzacs and the turbans of the Indians.

During the course of the war British units started wearing coloured identification patches, at first on the back of the tunic and later on the upper sleeves. In the following years this practice developed into a new form of military heraldry that was adopted by most of the world's armies.

Some European nations, when confronted by the necessity of camouflaging their soldiers, opted for grey or greenish materials in the belief that such colours would blend ideally in the Continental landscape: no one could have foreseen the years of muddy trench warfare that lay ahead.

Pike-grey was chosen by the Austro-Hungarians in 1907 and units were fitted

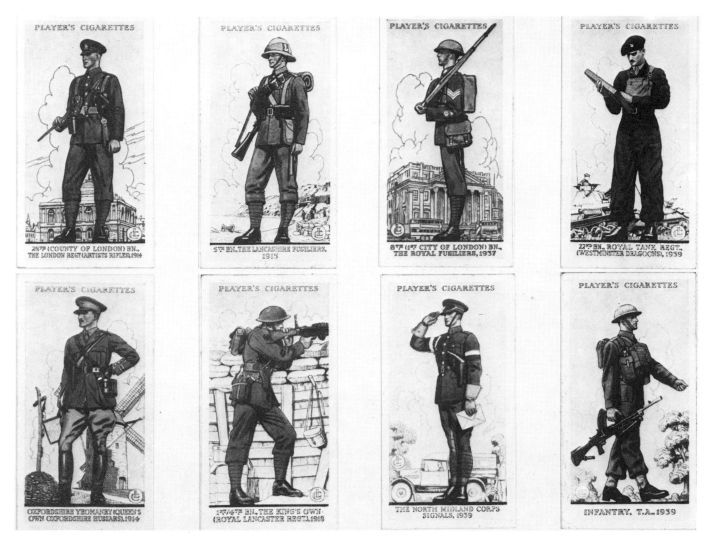

A set of cigarette cards
showing the uniforms of the
Territorial Army, 1937.

with the new field uniforms in the following years. These uniforms followed the basic pattern of the coloured uniforms, which were upgraded to the status of walking-out and parade dress. National and regimental dress distinctions were retained as much as possible and Bosnian Muslims, for example, were issued with their traditional tasselled fez. The officers wore the typical Austrian *képi* with black leather chin strap and visor, or a soft cap with folded sides similar to that of the soldiers. The steel helmet of German pattern came into use in 1916.

FRANCE

Infantryman, 1914   Infantryman, 1915–18   Lieutenant in marching kit, 1918   Cuirassier Officer, 1914   Infantryman of the Polish Haller Legion in the French service, 1916

GREAT BRITAIN

Hussar of the 13th Hussar Regiment   Fusilier of the Royal Fusiliers Regiment, 1914   Lancer, 1918   *Australia*, Sergent of Field Artillery, 1917   Infantryman, 1916

RUSSIA
Officer of the Field
Artillery, 1914

Infantryman, 1914

Cavalryman, 1914

Infantry Officer, 1917

Rumanian Infantryman,
1916

USA, Infantry Officer,
1917

BELGIUM, Infantryman,
1914

BELGIUM, Infantryman,
1918

ITALY, Bersagliere, 1915

ITALY, Infantry Officer,
1916

A group of Austrian officers in a photograph taken at Görz on the Southern Front in October 1915.

The single-breasted tunic originally did not show any buttons; it had four pockets with inner lining and typical Austrian large three-pointed flaps; also a stand-up collar with coloured patches that carried rank and branch of service insignia. The officer's tunic had no shoulder straps and was noticeably short; the soldier's tunic had its right shoulder strap rolled up at the outer end in order to prevent the rifle strap from slipping.

Field grey uniforms were issued from 1915 onwards and stand-and-fall collars became standard pattern for the tunic of all ranks, and also later issues of officers' pike-grey tunics were made with the new collar. In 1917 the other ranks' collar patches were replaced by a narrow vertical strip of coloured felt attached behind the rank and branch of service insignia. Patches with units' numbers and initials were adopted in the same year for wearing on the cap and shoulder straps of tunics and great-coats. Metal badges were worn by all ranks on the cap; all were unofficial and commemorated formations and battles in which the wearer had taken part.

Field uniforms were adopted in Prussia in February 1907: initially field grey uniforms were issued to the infantrymen and engineers and grey-green ones to the personnel of rifle regiments (*Jäger* and *Schüt-*

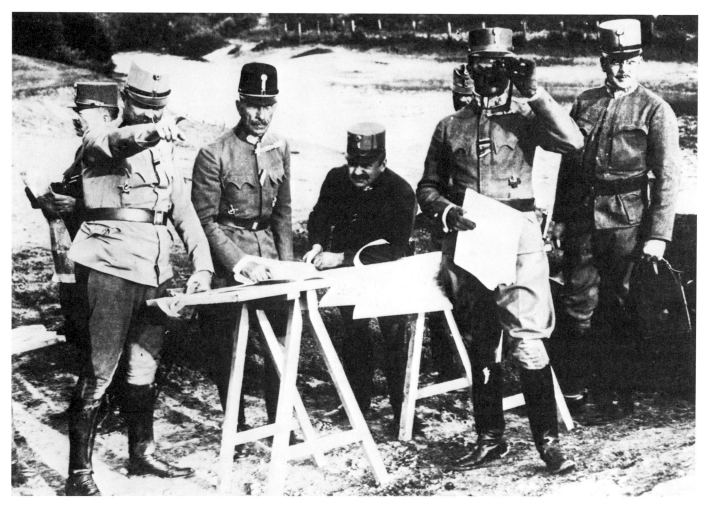

zen) and machine-gunners only. The artillery were given field grey uniforms in November, dragoons and lancers during the following year. Eventually, by 1910, all personnel of the Prussian army possessed the new field uniform and the armies of other German states followed suit. These, however, were replicas of the coloured uniforms with piping, lace, arm and regimental trimmings, but made of field grey or grey-green cloth. Cavalry regiments wore *attila-* and *ulanka-* type tunics and the collar, cuffs and back skirt flaps of standard-type tunics varied according to regimental tradition. Officers and sergeants wore a peaked cap with two cockades, the black,

white and red national cockade at the top and the state cockade below, on the cap band, while other ranks wore a peakless round cap with the usual cockades. Coloured cap bands were removed or covered by a field grey strap during the course of the war. The *Pickelhaube*, the riflemen's shako and the cavalry's traditional head-dresses were worn on the battlefield with an additional grey cover until 1916 when the steel helmet became general issue.

A new uniform of simplified, universal pattern was adopted in 1915: the new single-breasted buttonless tunic had stand-and-fall collar, hip pockets only, like the

The Austro-German capture of Czernowitz (Bukorma) from the Russians. The battle headquarters of the Austrian army Commander, General Boehim-Ermolli, on 3 August 1917.

previous one, but without any trimmings on the cuffs and back skirt and piping limited to the shoulder straps only. Officers were advised to wear the soldiers' uniforms to avoid unnecessary losses in the field. However, special cuffs were often added onto this tunic or, vice versa, old tunics with front buttons were issued, but devoid of cuffs and coloured shoulder straps.

As the war dragged on, the uniforms of the Austro-German armies became drabber and drabber as the quality of materials and leather rapidly deteriorated. Jackboots were replaced by puttees or canvas anklets and even the standard of badges, officers' lace and shoulder cords deteriorated.

The Italian troops in the colonies were issued with khaki field uniforms in 1887–9 but grey-green was chosen in 1906 as a more suitable colour for the uniforms of the troops in the metropolitan territory, and this was officially adopted three years later.

All the officers wore basically the same uniform, with four pockets on the tunic, while the other ranks were issued with different ones depending if they were on foot, on horse, cyclist or alpine troops. Most servicemen wore a soft *képi* with black leather visor and wide chin strap, but cavalrymen wore helmets or busbies according to speciality, *Bersaglieri* and *Alpini* wore their own typical hats. The tunics had concealed buttons, no pockets except for mounted troops and cyclists and the latter had stand-and-fall collar, while the tunic of all the other troops had a narrow stand-up collar with coloured patches and five-pointed white metal stars at the front. The soldiers on foot had a tunic with shoulder pads, while the tunics of the others carried shoulder straps and mounted troops had a short belt at the back of their tunic. Trousers with puttees or breeches with leggings were used by foot or mounted soldiers and equipment

also varied accordingly. The French steel helmet was adopted in 1916 and at about the same time a new rounded felt cap, nick-named the 'cup', started to be issued to the troops.

However, the most interesting developments in the field of uniforms are connected with the war-raised assault units: in about 1917 the personnel of these units decided to open up the collar of their tunics in accordance with civilian fashion. On the collar they wore two-pointed black collar patches with the usual star and favoured a black fez with tassel as their head-dress.

Portugal entered the conflict in March 1916 and subsequently sent an expeditionary force to the Western Front. All the Portuguese troops wore grey field uniforms modelled on the British pattern of that time: the men had peaked caps with cloth visors reinforced by lines of stitches, or the typical Portuguese helmet, similar in shape to the British one but with scalloped crown. They used British field webbing equipment in order to simplify supplies.

In August 1916 Rumania joined the cause of the Entente: its men wore grey uniforms and steel helmets of French pattern. The officers wore round *képis* of French style while the soldiers had caps with cloth visor and folded sides piped in arm-of-service colours. The tunics were single-breasted, with concealed buttons, four pockets and rank insignia on the shoulder straps; the stand-and-fall collar carried the typical Rumanian spearhead-shaped coloured patches.

The outbreak of the First World War caught the Belgians militarily unprepared, still with obsolete uniforms and rather impractical equipment. General mobilization was declared on 1 August 1914 but defeat was inevitable. Subsequently the Belgian army was reorganized and in March 1915 it was issued with khaki field

The regulation French infantry dress, photographed at the Army Clothing Department at Vanves, on 28 December 1916.

Russian officers and men on
board a transport ship in
South Russia, September
1918.

uniforms and French steel helmets with the Belgian Lion's head at the front. The uniform and the equipment were very similar to those of the British army, although the Belgian tunic had a stand-up collar with coloured patches and detachable shoulder straps with two buttons. The trousers were tucked into high laced boots or puttees.

The US army officially adopted khaki uniforms in 1902 and photographs of General Pershing and his staff on their arrival in Britain in June 1917 show the officers wearing peaked caps with brown leather visor and chin strap, a tunic with five front buttons, stand-up collar with US initials and branch badges on both sides and four patch pockets with flap but without pleats. They wore then a plain leather waist belt, later replaced by the British Sam Browne belt, and all the badges and buttons, except rank insignia, of officers and soldiers were bronzed. The soldiers' uniform was similar in style to that of the officers: they wore webbing equipment and canvas leggings or puttees.

The distinctive American head-dress was the wide-brimmed campaign hat, made of beaver-coloured felt, with a cord ending with acorns in arm-of-service colours for soldiers or in gold for officers. Later the overseas cap, a more practical forage cap, widely replaced the former. In 1917 the American troops were issued with French or British steel helmets but they eventually settled for the latter which they used until the early 1940s.

In the summer of 1914 the French army entered the battlefield with coloured uniforms: the infantryman, for example, wore blue tunic and greatcoat, dark red trousers, black leather field equipment, boots and gaiters. A bluish-grey cover was issued at the eleventh hour to fit over the red and blue *képi*. Cuirassiers went into battle with helmet and cuirass hidden by a cloth cover, blue tunics and red breeches. But although their clothing was obsolete, these men were armed with great courage and determination and soon checked the German advance.

Bluish-grey field uniforms, of a shade known as horizon-blue, were issued during the following year and brown, natural leather equipment was distributed later during the course of the war. *Chasseurs à pied* and *Alpins* wore the new horizon-blue greatcoat on their old blue and grey uniforms, colonial infantry and artillery wore horizon-blue uniforms while the African troops, *Zouaves*, Algerian, Moroccan and Senegalese Rifles, *Spahis* and African *Chasseurs* were dressed in khaki uniforms.

The *Poilu* wore a single-breasted tunic, trousers and puttees and the well-known greatcoat with large stand-and-fall collar and the front tails buttoned up at the back. The French were the first to adopt the steel helmet, the type known as the Adrian helmet.

The experience gained by the Russians during the 1904–5 War against Japan impelled their general staff to modernize the army and khaki field uniforms were introduced subsequently. The officers' uniform comprised a peaked cap, a single-breasted tunic with five buttons and stand-up collar, gold or silver lace shoulder boards and four pockets, tight breeches and riding boots. Cossacks were allowed their own traditional uniforms with fur caps and cavalrymen had blue breeches. The soldiers wore initially a sailor-type cap to which was later added a short peak; French-type helmets were adopted in theory but were never supplied to the whole army. Their most typical garment was the *gymnasterka*, a rather short shirt-tunic with a stand-up collar fastened by two buttons and three small buttons down the front, shirt-type cuffs and shoulder boards. Trousers or breeches and jackboots completed this outfit. Heavier clothing was used in winter, with long-length greatcoats and fur hats, the latter being standard head-dress for Cossacks and Siberian troops. The belt and ammunition pouches were made of brown leather.

The shoulder boards identified the rank, branch of service and regiment of the wearer by means of stars, NCOs' stripes, numbers, initials and badges, which were in silver on gold boards, or vice versa, for officers, and in arm-of-service colours for soldiers. The colours of the greatcoat's collar patches identified divisional regiments.

The Bulgarians followed the Russian fashion in the style of their uniforms and the Montenegrins and Serbians also adopted khaki uniforms with Russian features, but the latter kept their typical *képi*-shaped head-dress and Austrian type three-pointed pocket flaps.

The Turkish army adopted khaki field uniforms in about 1909, with fur hats for officers and mounted troops and sun helmets for the others. Branch of service colours were shown on the collar and head-dress and officers wore German-style rank insignia.

Japan declared war on Germany on 23 August 1914, China and Siam in 1917 and consequently their armies adopted 'westernized' uniforms. The Japanese, however, had experimented with khaki field uniforms since the Russo-Japanese War, uniforms which remained in use until 1930.

Red flags, red armlets and the red star, initially with a hammer and plough in its centre, later replaced by the well-known hammer and sickle, became the symbols of the 1917 Russian Revolution. The Tsarist shoulder boards were abolished as a symbol of privilege and red stars above red diamonds, squares or triangles according to class of rank, were worn on the lower sleeves instead. Also the conventional rank titles were replaced by direct denominations of command, for example commander of regiment, battalion, and so on.

A new head-dress, the *budionowka* was officially adopted in 1919; it was named after General Budienny whose troops were the first to wear it. The red star was pinned at the front on a larger cloth star in branch of service colour. During those troubled years the soldiers wore their old uniforms or anything they could find. New uniforms, badges and new rank insignia were introduced in 1922 and the latter were finally moved onto the collar patches two years later.

New nations were struggling for independence within the collapsing empires: Finland and the Baltic States gained independence from Russia; Czechoslovakia, Hungary and Yugoslavia emerged from the territory of the former Austro-Hungarian Empire and Poland reappeared on the map of Central Europe.

Many Finnish volunteers trained in the German army during the war and formed the 27th *Jäger* Battalion which in February 1918 was sent to Finland where, together with German troops, it helped the local patriots to expel the Russians. It is not surprising therefore that in 1922 the Finns opted for grey uniforms, which were modified in 1927 and again later, in 1936.

The Poles saw in the First World War the opportunity for achieving their long-lost national independence and acted accordingly, but in different ways, as individuals thought that this purpose could be secured by supporting one or the other cause. Polish legions were raised in France, in the Austro-Hungarian Empire, in Germany and of course. Poles also served in the Russian army. Czechoslovaks, mainly prisoners of war, were also recruited into legions in France, in Italy and in Russia. Both nations later adopted khaki uniforms

The Revolution in
Petrograd. Soldiers pictured
travelling on the footboard
of a motor-car with red flags
fixed to their bayonets.

and so did the Magyars but their uniforms still followed the Austrian fashion to which they were accustomed.

In December 1918 Yugoslavia became an independent nation composed of Slovenes, Croats and Serbs, although the former two peoples had previously been under Austrian rule, while the Serbs fought on the side of the Entente. The appearance of the new Yugoslav uniforms reflected the merging of these two different military traditions, as features were taken from one or from the other. The uniforms were field grey in accordance with Central European fashion, with Serbian-styled head-dress for all except guards who wore peaked caps, and gold shoulder boards for officers; generals, however, wore shoulder cords and six-pointed stars above the sleeve cuffs.

An aftermath of revolutions, civil wars and endless border disputes shocked Europe from the Baltic to the Adriatic. Left-wing parties sprang up everywhere and were counterbalanced by organizations of the right. In Italy, a militant association known as *Fasci di combattimento* was formed at Milan on 23 March 1919. The word *fascio*, or bundle, had been used for years in lieu of the term union, or association. In turn, this ideology, which eventually took over power in Italy, became known as Fascism.

The Fascist party black uniform consisted of a fez with tassel, jacket without lapels or buttons kept closed by a black Sam Browne belt, breeches and riding boots. Militiamen wore the fez, grey-green army-type uniforms, but with a jacket with open collar, which in those days was a great step forward in other ranks' dress.

Later, in the mid-1930s, a jacket with open collar was also adopted by the German *SS*, but except for the collar these uniforms were similar in style to the army pattern.

Italian Fascism and German National Socialism were drawn together by the Spanish Civil War and tragically, step by step, the world moved towards another major conflict.

The Second World War 1939-45

9

GUIDO ROSIGNOLI

Peacetime brought no major political upheavals to Britain but nevertheless national financial difficulties were evident. Cuts in the military budget caused several regimental amalgamations in the 1920s and uniforms were not changed for almost two decades. In 1936 a dark blue walking-out uniform was authorized for the occasion of George VI's coronation, but as a general rule the men made do with the old khaki field/service dress, accompanied by the webbing belt, which on its own appeared rather out of place. Individual soldiers cut off the bottoms of their trousers just below the top of the puttees in a supreme effort to appear smarter on the parade ground.

A new khaki field uniform, known as the battledress, and new webbing equipment, were introduced in 1937. The battledress comprised a short blouse with stand-and-fall collar and patch pockets on the chest, which was buttoned on to the trousers; the latter had back and side inner pockets and two patch pockets at the front, a large one with flap on the left thigh and a smaller one with pleats on the right hip, for the field dressing pack. The steel helmet, the forage cap with folded sides, webbing equipment, anklets and leather boots completed this uniform. At least two patterns of blouse were issued; one showed all the buttons while the better-quality blouse had the front and pocket buttonholes on inner linings.

Officers could wear the peaked cap and a pistol holster and ammunition pouch attached to the belt, the whole made of webbing material. Often the M 1908 webbing equipment was issued with the new battledress, or vice versa, as the old khaki uniform continued to be made for years, later for issue to the home forces. Tankmen, paratroopers and commandos wore black, maroon and dark green berets respectively,

and in 1943 khaki berets were issued to the remainder of the army.

Bush jackets and long trousers or shorts of light khaki drill cloth were worn in hot climates with forage cap, beret, Wolseley or steel helmet, according to specific duty. The bush jacket had a shirt-type collar and cuffs, four plain patch pockets with flaps and a cloth waist belt. Olive-green bush jackets and trousers were later worn in the Far East with Australian-type slouch hats. The shorts, usually worn with shirt only, were rather baggy, had side pockets and the usual field dressing pocket on the right hip. They were fastened at the front by two straps fixed by obtrusive little buckles.

Different, round steel helmets were used by parachutists and motorcyclists and special overalls were worn by tankmen; woollen pullovers, brown leather jerkins and greatcoats were worn in winter.

In Germany, the uniforms of the *Reichswehr* remained basically the same as previously but all the badges were changed after the First World War. In February 1919, for example, the rank insignia were moved onto the left sleeve and later onto both sleeves. Collar badges for all ranks were adopted in May of the same year and thin silver shoulder cords were used until January 1921, when the usual shoulder straps were reintroduced. The chin strap cords appeared in 1927.

Other modifications were introduced after 1933 when National Socialism came to power and finally, in 1936, totally different new uniforms were introduced: field grey dress and field/service uniforms and a special black uniform for armoured personnel. A field grey uniform, but cut in the style of the latter, was issued to personnel of tank destroyer and self-propelled assault gun units. The field grey tunic had dark bluish-green stand-up collar with patches and shoulder straps, four patch pockets

with flaps and pleats; the trousers, tucked into jackboots, were slightly darker. The dress uniform carried additional piping, collar double bars in arm-of-service colour and similar patches with a button on the cuffs. A smaller steel helmet was adopted in 1935 and a different helmet was used by parachutists. Other head-dresses were the peaked cap, the forage cap with folded sides and the mountain troops' cap with an additional soft peak, which later in the war was issued to the whole army. Tankmen initially wore a padded beret; later they sported

a black forage cap.

As the war spread to the steppes of Russia and to the North African desert, special winter clothing and light khaki uniforms were issued to the German troops, but as hostilities progressed the quality of the uniforms constantly deteriorated, until in 1944 a short blouse was issued in place of the field tunic, and boots with canvas anklets were worn instead of jackboots.

The *Waffen*-SS invented camouflage field clothing in the 1930s of which the Germans made extensive use during the war, and

A group of British soldiers of the battalion the Royal East Kent Regiment on 3 April 1940.

A group of Italian prisoners of war, 19 December 1940, in the North African desert. One of them insisted on taking his dog with him.

various types of camouflage uniforms, smocks, ponchos, overalls and helmet covers were issued to the troops. The colours varied to suit the seasonal landscape and often the garments were reversible, as another pattern was printed inside.

The Allies made only limited use of camouflage clothing; British paratroopers, for instance, wore the Denison smock-type jacket, the US Marines had a camouflage cover on the helmet, and some army units were issued temporarily with camouflage uniforms in Normandy. The Russians also made extensive use of white camouflage in winter and introduced coloured camouflage clothing after 1943.

The Second World War started on 3 September 1939 with the German attack on Poland. In the twenty years of its existence Poland had managed to build up an efficient army with regiments inspired by ancient traditions, reflected in their beautiful breast pocket badges. Polish troops wore khaki uniforms, adopted in 1936, of which the most typical item was the *chapska* (a peaked cap with square-shaped crown), although personnel of the light horse regiments and Frontier Defence Force had normal round peaked caps. Their tunics followed the fashion of the time, had four patch pockets with stand-and-fall collar and coloured patches of Polish pattern.

During the 1930s most armies reintroduced some form or another of ceremonial dress, especially the French who returned to the colourful regimental traditions of the past when in full dress or walking-out uniform. In 1935 khaki replaced the old *horizon bleu* of the field uniforms for all except *Chasseurs à pied* and *Alpins* who retained their dark blue tunics and grey-blue trousers. The officer's khaki service dress was technically divided into a *tenue de jour* and *tenue de travail* and worn with the characteristic coloured *képi*, while the *bonnet de police*, i.e. the forage cap, or the steel helmet, were worn with the field uniform. The generals had also a khaki *képi* with gold embroidered oak leaves on the chin strap. The officer's tunic had a rather small stand-and-fall collar with patches, French-type shoulder tabs, four pockets with flaps and seven buttons at the front, in gold or silver according to branch of service. They wore trousers or breeches, brown leather shoes or boots and Sam Browne belt. In the late 1930s they started to wear jackets with open collar.

The French soldiers were issued with walking-out and field uniforms: the former had coloured piping on the shoulder straps, coloured collar patches and NCOs' chevrons, and metal buttons while the field uniform had plain shoulder straps and patches, khaki buttons and short khaki stripes instead of chevrons. All ranks proudly wore regimental badges on the breast pockets.

The Belgians retained basically the 1915 uniforms although modifications were prescribed in the 1930s. By 1940 the officers and warrant officers wore British-style service dress, with peaked cap and jacket with open collar, while the other ranks wore tunics with collar patches, and numerals and badges on the shoulder straps. The *Chasseurs Ardennais* wore a large green beret with metal boar's head as cap badge.

The Italian army adopted new grey-green uniforms in 1934; all ranks were issued with jackets with an open collar and four patch pockets. *Képis* were substituted by peaked caps, or forage caps of typical Italian pattern. Cavalrymen, *Bersaglieri* and *Alpini* kept their traditional head-dresses and the *képi* continued to be worn by the horse artillery as parade head-dress. A new steel helmet was adopted in 1933.

All officers and the other ranks of mounted branches of service wore breeches while soldiers on foot were issued with 'plus-fours' and puttees. The equipment was the same as that used in the First World War, except that two ammunition pouches were issued instead of four. The troops in Africa wore similar uniforms but made of khaki material; a special jacket known as the *sahariana* was widely used in the colonies and later, in black, became the standard tunic of the Fascist party uniform. A similar jacket, but without collar and lapels, was worn by parachutists. In Italy, due to the variable climatic conditions, the grey-green uniform did not serve its purpose of 'a uniform for all seasons', as it was too hot for wearing in summer and even with additional vests and greatcoat it was never warm enough in winter.

During the Second World War most European nations eventually became involved in the conflict. In the North, a confrontation between Finland and Russia took place in the winter 1939–40, and continued after 1941, following on the German attack on the USSR. The Finnish uniforms were similar to the Germans' and German steel helmets were also used by the Finns, although there was no political affinity but purely a practical alliance between the two countries.

In 1940, for strategic reasons, Germany occupied Norway, Denmark and Holland, peace-loving nations that were caught quite unprepared. The Norwegian army adopted field uniforms in 1912 which were modified in 1934 but both the old and the new pattern were still in use in 1940. The uniforms were field grey, with green piping; rank

OVERPAGE American infantrymen of the 87th Division, enter the town of St Hubert, Belgium, immediately after the Germans fled the town in 1945.

stripes were worn on the *képi* and five-pointed stars on their own or combined with silver or gold lace stripes, according to class of rank, were displayed on the tunic's collar or shoulder straps of the greatcoat. The tunic had no shoulder straps and was worn with breeches or long trousers. Soldiers were issued with rucksacks and brown leather field equipment, which included two large ammunition pouches, while the officers had the pistol holster and a dual ammunition pouch only, attached to the Sam Browne belt. A cap with cloth visor and folded sides was used by all ranks for field duties.

The Danes adopted grey uniforms in 1915 but eight years later changed to khaki and in the same year, 1923, adopted their own typical steel helmet. Officers wore peaked cap and forage cap while soldiers had only the latter. Rank insignia were worn on the shoulder straps and branch of service badges on the collar of the tunic; corporals wore chevrons on the upper sleeves. Distinguishing coloured silk woven lace was worn on the shoulder straps and on the forage cap.

Grey-green uniforms were adopted by the Royal Netherlands Army in 1912 but during the following two years their colour was changed to field grey. By 1940 the standard field uniform consisted of a tunic with stand-up collar edged in arm-of-service colour, with branch badges and rank insignia in the case of officers and warrant officers, while NCOs wore chevrons above the cuffs. Officers and mounted soldiers wore breeches with leggings, or the former, with riding boots; infantrymen had trousers with puttees. Generals wore peaked caps, while all the other ranks wore *képis*, forage caps or the steel helmet, according to duty.

The Dutch had an independent military organization in their colonies, the Royal Netherlands Indian Army, which had different uniforms, with different badges. Rank was identified by collar patches and bronze branch badges were worn on the tunic's shoulder straps. Peaked caps, slouch hats or helmets were commonly used with field dress while the *képi* was worn with white or dark uniforms only.

In June 1941 Germany attacked the Soviet Union, the army of which was going through a process of reorganization after the Winter War with Finland. The khaki uniforms in use at that time had been introduced in 1935, although modified in 1940 when special uniforms were adopted for marshals and generals, and rank badges were up-dated. The khaki field uniform comprised the peaked cap, or forage cap, or steel helmet or a fur hat in winter; the typical Russian shirt-tunic (*gymnasterka*) with breast pockets only, trousers or breeches and jackboots. Greatcoats, padded and fur-lined garments were used in winter. Tank troops wore steel-grey uniforms and special overalls and Cossacks, when possible, kept alive their traditions by wearing at least their astrakhan caps with the drab field uniforms.

New uniforms were adopted in 1943 and the shirt-tunic was modified as well: the breast pockets were eliminated, the collar was changed to a stand-up pattern and buttons were added on the front. But by far the most important innovation was the reintroduction of shoulder boards as marks of command: those for field uniform were khaki edged in arm-of-service colour and with one or two longitudinal dark red stripes along the centre in the case of junior and senior officers, respectively. NCOs had dark red stripes across their khaki shoulder boards and gold lace boards were used by marshals, generals and also by officers on uniforms other than field.

Hungary, Rumania and Bulgaria took the side of Germany and their armies fought on the battlefields of the Eastern Front. All wore khaki uniforms: the appearance of the Hungarian uniforms echoed the former imperial style. Their collar patches were particularly interesting as they were ornamented with the traditional Hungarian twisted braiding. The Rumanians adopted khaki uniforms in the 1920s and during the following decade chose to follow the British fashion. Officers wore peaked caps and jackets with open collar. Bulgarian uniforms retained an old Tsarist Russian appearance to which some Germanic features were added in the late 1930s. The Bulgarian peaked cap, for instance, was typically Russian, with an oval cockade at the front; officers wore Russian-type shoulder boards with German-type square 'pips', and double bars on the tunic's collar.

The Americans were provided with elegant and sensible uniforms and brought to Europe a new fashion in military dress, which influenced civilian fashion as well. They lowered the waist-height of the trousers and replaced the braces with trouser belts. Americans were issued with winter and summer uniforms and wore a variety of field uniforms according to season and type of duty.

In north-west Europe the average soldier wore khaki (olive-drab) shirt and trousers and a short weatherproof olive green field jacket with zip fastener and buttons. The latter replaced the khaki jacket with patch pockets of the service dress. The woollen field jacket, OD (olive-drab), which was technically a blouse with open collar and breast patch pockets, was adopted in 1944 and eventually replaced the previously mentioned service jacket. In the field it was worn under a windproof, water repellent jacket, olive-green in colour, with open collar, four pockets and an inner tightening string around the waist.

A new helmet was devised in 1941: it consisted of a fibre-lined helmet on which the steel helmet proper could be fitted; a woollen knitted cap could be worn beneath in cold weather. The peaked cap and the overseas cap, the latter by then known as the 'garrison cap', were usually worn with service dress, while the wide-brimmed campaign hat disappeared during the course of the war. Green field webbing equipment was a development (1936) of the former 1912 pattern and canvas leggings were eventually replaced by russet leather boots with integral anklets with two side buckles, or laced up for paratroopers.

Paratroopers and tankmen were issued with different field clothing and special garments were issued for particular assignments and to cope with unusual climatic conditions. The olive-green cotton fatigue uniform, with large breast and hip patch pockets, was widely used as a combat uniform as well and after many trials and experiments, conducted by the US army, navy, and Marine Corps in the Pacific Theatre, it developed eventually into the modern, functional American field uniform. The attacking Japanese armies found the GIs dressed in light khaki shirt and trousers summer uniforms which continued to be used for well over a decade; the flaps of the shirt pockets were then cut away at the corners.

The Japanese M 98 uniform was adopted in 1938, and was a modification of the M 90, adopted eight years earlier. On the latter, the rank badges were worn as shoulder tabs and patches were displayed on the collar, while from 1938 onwards the rank insignia replaced the collar patches. Their uniforms were khaki of varying shades: the most common head-dress was a rounded cap with cloth visor and brown leather chin strap or the steel helmet. The tunic had a stand-and-fall collar and four pockets; trousers or

GERMANY
Cavalry Officer, 1943

Paratrooper, 1940

Artillery Officer of the
Afrika Corps, 1941

Infantryman, 1940

Panzer Trooper, 1940

RUMANIA,
Infantryman, 1941

BULGARIA,
Infantryman, 1941

ITALY,
Brigadier-General in
North Africa, 1941

ITALY, Infantryman,
1940

ITALY, Paratrooper,
1943

HUNGARY,
Infantryman, 1941

FINLAND, Infantryman,
1941

JAPAN, Officer, 1942

JAPAN, Infantryman,
1943

JAPAN, armoured troops,
1942

GREECE, Infantryman,
1940

POLAND, Sergeant of
the 1st Infantry Division
(Tadeusz Kosciusko's),
1945

YUGOSLAVIA,
Sergeant-Major of
Cavalry, 1940

GERMANY – NCO of
the Cossack Division
(Don Cossacks), 1944

SLOVAKIA,
Infantryman, 1942

breeches were tucked in puttees and the field equipment was made partly of leather and partly of canvas. As the conquering Japanese armies spread all over Asia their lines of communications became longer and thinner, and when the Allies counterattacked, the Japanese garrisons became lost in the Pacific islands, in the jungles of the Far East and in the vastness of China. Soldiers made do with what clothing they could find locally.

In the early 1940s European monarchs, politicians, soldiers and civilians escaped to Britain and there formed governments 'in exile' and raised their own armed forces dressed and equipped by the War Office. The Germans also recruited foreigners in autonomous formations which, however, were part of the German armed forces. All wore German uniforms with their own special badges, or even national items of dress, for instance the Cossacks who wore astrakhan hats, or Indians who wore turbans.

Yugoslavia was soon torn apart by civil strife among monarchist Chetniks, Croatian Ustashe and Tito's communists; all wore the uniforms and arms of the nation that supported them and, after 1943, when Italy collapsed, all made use of captured Italian equipment. Civil war then began in northern Italy between the partisans supported by the Allies and the Fascists, backed by the Germans. The Black Brigades were particularly involved in antipartisan warfare: their uniform varied considerably but most men wore black shirts and displayed various skull-and-cross-bones badges as well as conventional Fascist insignia.

In Europe the war ended on 5 May 1945 and Japan, the last of Germany's allies, capitulated on 15 August 1945 after atomic bombs had been dropped on Hiroshima and Nagasaki.

ABOVE A German officer and his men surrender to Canadian troops after the Normandy landings in 1944.

RIGHT A group of Chetniks of the Yugoslav army pictured on the Adriatic coast. After the collapse of Italy in 1943, they made use of captured Italian equipment.

FRANCE, Infantry, 1940

POLAND, Infantryman, 1939

POLAND, Cavalryman, 1939

FRANCE, Officer of the Alpine Chasseurs

NORTH AFRICA, Legionary of the Foreign Legion, 1941

ENGLAND, Infantryman, 1944

ENGLAND, Staff Officer in North Africa, 1942

AUSTRALIA, Infantryman (Far East), 1944

NORWAY, Infantryman, 1940

DENMARK, Infantryman, 1940

HOLLAND, Infantryman, 1940

BELGIUM, Armoured troops, 1940

RUSSIA, General, 1943

RUSSIA, Armoured troops, 1941

RUSSIA, Infantryman, 1943

USA, Infantryman, 1943

USA, Sergeant of the 2nd Armoured Division, 1945

USA, Infantry Corporal, 1942

CHINA, Infantryman, of the Nationalist Army, 1943

CHINA, Infantryman, of the Red Army, 1943

10

The Armies of the Atomic Age – the World after 1945

GUIDO ROSIGNOLI

After the Allied victory of 1945 European armies were gradually reduced in size and structurally reorganized. They have continued to be reorganized periodically since then to meet the changing requirements of new weapons, constantly fluctuating strategic and tactical conditions and the financial limitations imposed by economic and political pressures. Equipment and uniforms have continued to be modified to meet these changes.

The issue of the magazine *Soldier* of 28 April 1945 reported the introduction of the 1944 pattern of webbing equipment for the British Army 'which will become a general issue in all theatres as present stocks wear out'. The new equipment was olive green and was light in weight due to finer webbing and alloy buckles and clips; therefore, although it comprised larger pouches and a double-capacity haversack, it was still lighter to carry than the 1937 pattern. The belt incorporated a series of metal-rimmed holes for hanging items of equipment that previously had to be carried in the haversack or pouches and the new water bottle was combined at last with a cup. The new helmet with sloping back was adopted at the same time.

A new green jungle suit, primarily devised for use in the Far East, was reported in November of the same year; the jacket had two breast pockets, the trousers had six: two side and two bellows pockets, one on the thigh and one for the field dressing. The brimmed jungle hat, the jersey pullover with patches on the shoulders and elbows, a new lightweight blanket, the poncho, a rucksack and other new items were also introduced. The poncho replaced both the groundsheet and gas cape and could be used as a raincoat, sleeping bag or one-man tent and a larger tent could be built by fastening a number of ponchos together.

Although these new items were experimented with during the war and were later issued to units in Java and Malaya, the ubiquitous battledress, used as field uniform and service dress with or without field equipment, remained unchanged until 1949, when a new blouse with collar and lapels was authorized and the trousers' hip pocket was eliminated. By then a new dark blue beret, or one in traditional colours for certain regiments, had replaced the wartime khaki pattern.

In the late 1940s the American GI became the most elegant soldier in the world. His winter khaki, known as olive drab, walking-out uniform consisted of the forage cap (garrison cap) or peaked cap, the blouse (field, wool, OD) showing khaki shirt and tie, trousers and shoes or trousers tucked into the boots' integral anklets. The pocket flaps were often sewn down, various devices were used to keep the shirt collar straight and the olive-green water repellent jacket was often taken in around the waist for the sake of elegance.

A woollen khaki shirt could be worn without the blouse in mild weather, while in hot summer climates the GI wore light, sandy khaki garrison cap, shirt with the tie folded in between the second and third buttons, trousers, and footwear already described. The summer uniforms were heavily starched and vertical lines were creased in by ironing at the front and back of the shirt.

Shiny helmets with colourful badges, weapons and webbing waist-belt with pouches were worn on parade and later, silk scarfs in arm of service colours also appeared. Honour guards, bands and military policemen were particularly impressive.

The wartime olive-green field and work uniforms with large breast and hip pockets continued to be worn, together with the water repellent jacket in winter, or other

ENGLAND,
Infantryman, 1949

ENGLAND, Officer of
the Argyll and Sutherland
Highlanders, 1950

ENGLAND, Corporal of
the Royal Corps of
Pioneers, 1973

BELGIUM, Paratrooper,
1952

NORWAY, Infantryman,
1962

FRANCE, Infantryman,
1953

FRANCE, Paratrooper,
1961

FRANCE, Infantryman in
combat suit, 1954

ITALY, Alpini, 1960

ITALY, Infantryman,
1960

WEST GERMANY,
Infantryman in combat
suit, 1956

USA, Infantryman, 1950

TURKEY,
Sergeant-Major of
Infantry, 1962

WEST GERMANY,
Mountain Chasseur,
1964

USA, Soldier of the 1st
Cavalry Division, 1968–9

SWITZERLAND,
Infantryman, 1975

SPAIN, Officer, 1958

SWEDEN, UNO troops
(Gaza), 1961

AUSTRIA, Infantryman
in summer combat suit,
1974

FINLAND, Infantry,
1969

The American 351st Infantry Regiment marching through a town in southern Europe. In the late 1940s the American GI became the most elegant soldier in the world.

garments, for instance the zippered blouse with woollen collar and waistband or the short olive-green overcoat with side pockets, which were already used by special troops, or in cold weather. Fur-lined, hooded parkas and fur hats were used by American troops in extremely cold climatic conditions. Greatcoats were eventually replaced by a heavy green raincoat and by the utility garments described above.

The Russians, who occupied half of Europe, not to be outdone by the Americans, introduced new parade/walking-out uniforms from 1945 onwards: initially bottle-green uniforms were adopted for marshals and generals and in 1949 the other officers were given suits with double-breasted jackets and trousers in khaki or steel-grey, the latter for armoured personnel. The field uniform remained unchanged.

During the war both the British and the Americans supplied the French army, which politically was among the major Allied armed forces, and after the defeat of Germany, French troops were included in the army of occupation. A new range of uniforms was developed soon after the war and included a khaki service dress with a coloured *képi* for officers and warrant officers and coloured forage caps for the rank and file. The former wore jackets, the latter a battledress-type uniform with metal buttons on the blouse. Once again the *Chasseurs à pied* and *Alpins* chose dark blue instead of khaki. A new khaki greatcoat was introduced in 1947.

Light khaki shirt and trousers uniforms, with usual head-dress were worn in summer and olive-green field uniforms of American style made of drill or linen were adopted in 1947. Helmets of US pattern, French leather equipment and boots with anklets completed the field uniform.

The American and British armed forces embarked on the process of demobilization which led to internal unemployment; meanwhile the forces of occupation had to be maintained and bases had still to be manned, while troubles flared up across the world from the Adriatic to the Far East. Consequently National Service was reintroduced in Britain and lasted until 1960. While the major powers were streamlining their armies, the other nations that had been shattered during the course of the war were rebuilding theirs, a fact that led to the alliances of the late 1940s.

Belgian, Dutch, Danish and Norwegian forces took part in the liberation of their own countries and, as most then wore the British battledress, their post-war uniforms were modelled on the British pattern, although all eventually opted for American-type helmets.

The Belgians, for instance, have been among the most faithful followers of British fashion until the 1970s and continued to wear the khaki battledress but with an open collar carrying coloured patches, and British webbing equipment. They kept the war-time coloured berets, plus the floppy green one of the *Chasseurs ardennais* and appropriated some British badges which they had shared during the war: the paratroopers' Bellerophon and Pegasus, the commandos' dagger and the Parachute Regiment's and SAS wings. The Norwegians took home the British coloured branch of service strips which they continued wearing for years on the upper sleeves.

All wore their own national insignia; some changed to forage caps, others added buttons to the blouse or changed the pattern of the pocket flaps but the British battledress remained the inspiration of the uniforms of the 1940s. The Greek, Turkish and Italian armies adopted British battledress which was eventually modified to provide a national identity. The Italian-made battledress, for instance, had rectangular pocket flaps and no patch pockets on the trousers. Light shirt and trouser uniforms, with forage cap, were at last provided for summer.

Growing political instability led to the defence pact of March 1948 known as the Brussels Treaty, signed by Britain, France, Belgium, Holland and Luxemburg, which in turn gave birth to the North Atlantic Treaty Organization on 4 April 1949. In this new alliance the nations of the Brussels Treaty were joined by the United States, Canada, Denmark, Norway, Iceland, Italy and Portugal. Greece and Turkey joined NATO in 1952 and the German Federal Republic in 1955.

Both treaties led to the formation of headquarters organizations, the former to the HQ Western Europe Commanders-in-Chief, (the badge of which depicted five gold chain links on a blue pentagon) an organization that developed into the Supreme Headquarters Allied Powers Europe.

The necessity for new combat clothing became evident during the Korean War; combined NATO manoeuvres confirmed this view and marked the beginning of the slow process of standardization of field uniforms.

The new German *Bundeswehr* eliminated links with old traditions and went for the most modern clothing of that time: the first dress regulations, dated 23 July 1955, introduced grey service and walking-out uniforms, olive-green fatigue overalls and camouflage combat dress. Service and walking-out uniforms consisted of peaked cap, or soft cap with visor and folded sides, a remarkable double-breasted jacket with lapels, shorter for rank and file, trousers with shoes or tucked into boots' anklets. The fatigue uniform had American-type

EGYPT, Officer, 1952

ISRAEL, Infantryman, 1960

INDIA, Infantryman, 1952

NORTH KOREA, Officer, 1953

CHINA, Soldier of the Red Army, 1977

RUMANIA, Mountain Trooper, 1973

RUMANIA, Armoured Troops Officer, 1973

EAST GERMANY, Infantryman in combat suit, 1975

POLAND, Infantry Officer in summer combat suit, 1975

POLAND, Paratrooper, NCO

CZECHOSLOVAKIA,
Infantryman in summer
combat suit, 1973

CZECHOSLOVAKIA,
Infantryman in summer
combat suit, 1973

EAST GERMANY, 2nd
Lieutenant of the Rifles
(motorized), 1974–5

YUGOSLAVIA,
Mountain trooper, winter
combat suit, 1974

YUGOSLAVIA,
Infantryman, summer
combat suit, 1973–4

HUNGARY, Infantry
Officer in summer field
service uniform, 1974

HUNGARY, Armoured
trooper in winter
equipment, 1974

USSR, Infantry Officer,
1972

USSR, Airborne Trooper,
1972

USSR, Infantry
(motorized), 1972

patch pockets on the breast and trousers. The camouflage patchy-pattern combat dress consisted of a jacket with hood and four large patch pockets, trousers with leg pockets, camouflage gloves and black leather boots with anklets and side buckles, American pattern. The steel helmet was American too.

A more conventional single-breasted service jacket with traditional double bars on the collar was adopted in 1957 and other uniform details were changed subsequently.

In 1959 the camouflage dress was replaced by an olive-grey uniform issued in summer and winter variations and different versions for airborne, mountain and tank troops. The head-dresses in general use were the forage cap or the helmet, while paratroopers, tankmen, and later riflemen, wore berets, and mountain troops kept the old soft cap with peak. The uniform comprised a shirt, a tunic with breast pockets which could be tucked into the trousers, a jacket with breast pockets only, with or without hood, trousers tucked into jackboots, field equipment and steel helmet. White winter camouflage, parkas, overalls and other items of clothing were provided for special troops or in exceptional climatic conditions.

The Italian army opted for camouflàge field uniforms, composed of the steel helmet of Italian pattern, camouflage tunic with breast pockets only, trousers with side leg pockets, khaki webbing equipment and boots with webbing, later changed to leather integral anklets. The camouflage was worn above the basic uniform of summer or winter specification. Mountain troops were issued with olive-green jackets, khaki trousers, gaiters and mountain-type boots.

The Eastern European nations joined in a common military alliance known as the Warsaw Pact, in May 1955. The signatory countries were Albania, Bulgaria, Czechoslovakia, the German Democratic Republic, Hungary, Poland, Rumania and the Soviet Union. Albania left the alliance in 1968. These political developments led to the changing of many badges: red stars and communist symbols appeared while crowns and emblems of past regimes were abolished.

During the war Polish Liberation armies were raised in the West and in the East; the former wore British uniforms throughout the conflict while the latter, in the Soviet Union, adopted their own uniforms from about 1943 and developed them later, after the war. By 1945 their summer and winter uniforms, except for minor details were similar to those used before the war. The officers wore the *chapska* although the personnel of the Warsaw Division had peaked caps instead, the old tunic with typical Polish collar patches, breeches with riding boots or trousers and shoes. The soldiers wore soft caps with peak and folded sides, pre-war-type uniform with breeches and puttees or trousers tucked into webbing anklets. Tankmen were temporarily issued in the late 1940s with steel-grey uniforms in accordance with Soviet fashion. Leather waist-belt and ammunition pouches were worn in combination with other webbing equipment.

The *chapska* was gradually phased out and service dress jackets with open collar appeared in 1952; the new combat dress, made in field grey striped cloth in summer and winter versions, was adopted in 1958. The former consisted of the helmet, a jacket with four patch pockets and trousers tucked in the boots' integral anklets with two buckles on the side. The hip pockets of the jacket were later replaced by a single pocket on the left upper sleeve in accordance with East European fashion. Parachutists and other special troops had pockets on the trouser thighs, four pockets on summer and winter jackets and on both upper sleeves. In the early 1970s the striped pattern uniforms were replaced by similar ones made in olive-grey material of special texture with sleeve pocket on the winter jacket as well.

In January 1956 when the German Democratic Republic raised its National People's Army a great deal of care was taken to keep the new army's uniforms in line with German tradition, although the colour of the basic service dress was changed from field grey to stone-grey (a brownish shade of grey). Field uniforms were developed in line with Eastern fashion, from a patchy pattern of camouflage to grey in summer and winter versions. The summer field uniform was made with the typical Eastern field grey striped material and consist of a jacket with pocket flaps on the breast and upper sleeves and on both sides of the trouser legs. The winter field uniform had side pockets and sleeve pockets on the jacket, and pockets on the trousers as did the summer version. The new steel helmet, a forage cap or a fur hat could be worn according to duty and season and jackboots were worn with all but walking-out uniform. Paratroopers and tank crews wore different uniforms. Special shoulder straps with grey cords and lace were introduced recently for wearing on field uniforms.

Although a great deal of standardization has been achieved in Eastern Europe each nation has retained its individuality in the field of uniforms. The Czechoslovaks, for instance, adopted the striped field grey pattern, while others, such as the Rumanians, chose plain field grey combat dress; even field grey varies from a more or less brown to a greyish shade. Coloured patchy or white camouflage overalls are used by some armies according to climatic necessity or by

special troops, and black, bluish or grey overalls are usually worn by tankmen.

An interesting development in the post-war period has been the formation of United Nations Task Forces. At the first assembly of the United Nations Security Council held on 17 January 1946 a Military Staff Committee was formed to advise the Council on military matters and to supervise armed contingents put at its disposal by member nations in case of international emergencies. The Korean War was the first major emergency and UN Forces have subsequently intervened in many troubled areas all over the world. The men usually wear their national uniforms combined with blue head-dress and UNO badges.

The Korean War broke out on 25 June 1950 and American troops intervened less than a week later; they had the same uniform and equipment used during the Second World War, uniforms that proved inadequate during the harsh Korean winter.

The water repellent green jacket (field, M 1943) was the basis for similar zippered,

An East German soldier on army exercises. He is wearing the new steel helmet and field grey uniform adopted in 1956.

wool or fur-lined jackets which were issued, together with parka-type garments with integral or removable hood. Many of these items of winter clothing had been tested and used earlier: fur-lined caps with ear flaps and visor folded up were commonly used and a new white camouflage parka, over-trousers and Eskimo-type boots were experimented with in combat during the first winter. Bullet-proof vests and a new helmet were tested by some units in the following months but were never widely used.

A special winter kit was issued to the British troops in Korea in January 1951. It consisted basically of a windproof camouflage smock with hood, and trousers which were worn above the battledress; a soft cap with ear flaps and visor was worn below the hood and special shoes were also distributed, Finnish-style boots lined with felt and mud-resistant *boucheron* boots. A white kapok-filled coat with overlap wind-trap, cap comforter, white snow smock, trousers and gloves, green heavy woollen jersey and woollen underwear were part of the kit.

The French were just as unprepared to face the Korean winter, as initially all they could wear was the olive-green field uniform over the khaki battledress and the greatcoat on top. To simplify problems of supply, as in the case of other allied nations, the French were issued with American utility garments and webbing equipment. Regulations published in 1953 standardized the field uniforms into a general pattern for summer or winter wear, the latter with a jacket similar to the American M 1943 type; a mountain pattern in olive-green or white versions, a patchy camouflage combat suit with webbing equipment for airborne troops and special uniforms for motorized units and tank crews. A new steel helmet with plastic fibre liner was adopted in 1951 and another type, without liner, in 1974. In 1964 the French army adopted a new field uniform, similar to the previous pattern but made in windproof, anti-atomic cotton satin fabric composed of interchangeable linings, according to seasonal requirements.

The Korean experience revealed the impracticability of wearing garments one above the other in winter and therefore a great effort was made to design a combat dress for all seasons, with interchangeable inner layers of fabric. The Canadians, for instance, in 1953 had already tested a nylon combat suit based on this concept, which with an additional knee-length parka could be worn in near Arctic conditions.

The December 1957 issue of *Soldier* magazine described the newly adopted olive-green combat dress of the British army. It was an improved variation of the uniform already worn in Korea and included a new type of webbing equipment (1958 pattern). The suit consisted of a smock made of sateen fabric with water repellent lining and detachable hood, four pockets and 'poacher' pocket at the back, and trousers made of the same material. A parka finally replaced the greatcoat and a hooded nylon cape could be utilized as raincoat, or two could be made up into a tent. The new webbing equipment had four pouches, two on the sides and two behind, below the pack.

The old khaki battledress was on its way out: the following year new experimental walking-out uniforms were put on trial and one pattern was eventually adopted. It consisted of a head-dress in traditional colours and a suit, jacket and trousers made of khaki material.

At about the same time the US army discarded khaki, olive-drab, by adopting a new green-grey, technically known as 'Army Green', service dress composed of

garrison or peaked cap, jacket and trousers. The summer uniforms were modified also and in the mid 1950s berets were issued to the personnel of the Special Forces. This was a controversial decision at that time but other units also eventually adopted coloured berets.

In Vietnam the American soldiers wore tropical fatigues with jungle boots and only a few units, mainly airborne, Rangers and US Advisors, used patchy camouflage clothes, including the famous tiger suits. The modern field dress consists of the steel helmet with a new improved inner lining and camouflage cover, olive-green jacket similar to the previous pattern but without lapels, olive-green shirt and trousers, black gloves and boots. Various types of boots were experimented with including, recently, the 'Mickey Mouse' pattern.

A street barrier guarded by British soldiers in Northern Ireland.

Subdued insignia in black and olive-green, replaced the coloured insignia worn on the service dress. The webbing equipment, known as ALICE (All-Purpose Lightweight Individual Carrying Equipment) included belt and shoulder straps that carried two ammunition pouches, a smaller one for the field dressing, the bayonet, water bottle, spade and a larger pack at the back.

In the USSR a new field uniform, in summer and winter versions, was issued to the troops from 1970 onwards: its main feature was a new single-breasted tunic, with stand-and-fall collar and side pockets which replaced the traditional shirt-tunic.

Meanwhile a new experiment was taking place in the Far East. Rank insignia were abolished in the People's Liberation Army of China and everyone wore a standardized uniform: a visored soft cap, tunic and trousers, all in olive-green. A plain red star was worn on the cap and red patches, known as 'flags', on the tunic's collar.

Between 1971 and 1973 the range of clothing of the British soldier was finalized into four main categories, parade, combat, barracks dress and protective clothing, subdivided for temperate and warm weather climates. Now the military 'wardrobe' comprises sixteen orders of dress. The combat dress was devised on the layer system and includes patchy-pattern camouflage jacket and trousers combined with olive-green garments: shirt, quilted liner, woollen jersey, summer or winter underwear.

The army's involvement in civil unrest led to the adoption of some special items of equipment: as early as the mid-1950s in Cyprus the soldiers were issued with shields and wire mesh visors that could be fitted on the helmet and later, in Northern Ireland, more sophisticated anti-riot equipment was devised. A perspex visor was fitted to the helmet and a new transparent head-to-foot shield secured protection against shotguns and .22 weapons, together with bullet-proof vests. The search for an ideal body protection has never been abandoned and various experiments have taken place during this century; in the early 1940s the British army tested a three-piece armour plated suit and in the 1950s the 'Armadillo' suit was invented in America; it consisted of a series of laminated nylon plates attached to jacket and trousers.

In Britain during the 1950s the Mobile Defence Corps experimented with radiation-proof rubber gloves and boots, respirators and plastic capes but the constant fear of NBC (Nuclear Biological Chemical) warfare led to the invention of more and more elaborate and eerie protective clothing. The French tried large polythene bag-type overalls, others went for more conventional clothing made of special fabrics.

In fewer than seventy years, military fashion has progressed from red and blue to camouflage and the riflemen and gunners of the past have become highly skilled technicians. The line of development of future uniforms is vague as it is a contest between entirely new ideas and progressive improvements of old ones. The results are often surprising: The Bundeswehr adopted American steel helmets while the US army plan to adopt an improved variation of the much criticized German scuttle helmet.

We are now far from the days when uniforms were used as a means of distinguishing friend from foe on the battlefield and the modern soldier is often engaged in controlling civil unrest, an unfair role for a uniformed man. Perhaps, eventually, the wearing of uniform may be restricted to ceremonial occasions, and we will be back to the beginning, when the soldier possessed only one uniform.

Glossary

attila	hussar's tunic
bandolier	shoulder-belt with loops or pockets for cartridges
bayonet	stabbing blade attached to rifle-muzzle
bicorn hat	('millwheel'), cocked hat with brim turned up on two sides
bluse	loose, protecting over-garment
boucheron	buttoned boots
braid	embroidery of wool or metal
brandenbourgs	frogs and loops
breeches	short trousers fastened below the knee
budionowka	Russian head-dress (1919 onwards) with red star on the front
busby	tall fur cap of hussars and guardsmen
carbine	short firearm for cavalry use
cartouche box	cartridge box
casquette	(*Kaskett*) tall, tapering cap or shako
cassock	long coat
chapska	peaked cap with square-shaped crown
chemisette	a sleeved waistcoat
coatee	close-fitting short coat
cockade	rosette worn in hat as badge of office
confederatka	a form of *chapska* (qv)
contre-epaulette	epaulette strap without a fringe
couse	(halberd) combined spear and battle-axe
cravat	scarf, necktie
cuirass	body armour, breastplate and back-plate fastened together
demi-kaftan	short tunic
dolman	hussar's braided jacket
doublet	body-garment with or without sleeves and short skirts
dragoonka	small, round fur cap
epaulette	ornamental shoulder-piece of uniform
espontoon	pole weapon with an ornamental blade head
facing	turned back part of coat-tail; embellishments to uniform – cuff, collar, lapel, etc.
fasces	emblems of authority of Roman Lictors
flaps	pocket covers
flintlock musket	musket discharged by spark from flint
flounder	oval or square braided cord usually with a heavy tassel
flugel cap	(*mirliton*) winged cap
forage cap	('bonnet'), development of pointed civilian nightcap
frog	attachment to waist-belt to support sword or bayonet; ornamental coat fastening or spindle-shaped button and loop
fusil	light musket
gaiters	covering of cloth or leather for leg below the knee
Glengarry	Highland cap with pointed front and usually a pair of ribbons attached at back
gorget	piece of armour to protect the throat
gymnasterka	Russian shirt with side or centre opening
haversack	bag for provisions carried on the back or over one shoulder
hose	stockings
jerkin	sleeveless jacket
kaftan	double-breasted tunic
Kaskett	(*casquette*) tall, tapering cap or shako which could be lowered in bad weather
képi	French military cap with horizontal peak
kersey	tough, woollen cloth
khak	Hindustani word meaning 'dust'
khaki	dust-coloured uniform
Khevenhüller	Austrian hat, high-brimmed
kittel	Russian jacket
kiwer	Russian shako
klobuk	tall, cylindrical felt cap
knapsack	canvas or travelling bag, strapped to back
knickerbockers	loose-fitting breeches gathered in at the knee
Koller	jacket worn by cuirassiers
Kollern	German for the colouring of clothes with various earth colours
kolpak	bag of coloured cloth, originally the crown of a cap

kurtka	short waisted jacket with lapels forming a *plastron* with pointed cuffs
leggings	outer covering of leather etc. for leg, from knee to ankle
litzen	lace loops
mi-parti	contrasted colouring of the right and left halves of a garment
mirliton	(flugel cap) peakless shako with coloured cloth wing
moccasins	footwear of soft deerskin etc.
Muffer	small wig with pigtail
musket	infantry soldier's light gun
opanken	strips of leather wrapped round feet instead of shoes
pantaloons	loose linen trousers, overalls
parka	skin jacket with hood attached
pelisse	fur-lined mantle or cloak usually worn by hussars
pelzrock	pelisse
pickelhaube	spiked helmet
piping	ornamentation of uniform
plastron	breast-plate
Pluderhose	breeches
plus-fours	long, wide knickerbockers
puggaree	turban
puttee	long strip of cloth wound spirally round leg from ankle to knee
sabre-briquet	short-armed sword
sabretache	cavalry officer's flat satchel on long straps from the left shoulder or the waist-belt
sash	ornamental scarf worn over one shoulder or round waist
shako	more or less cylindrical hat with peak and upright plume or tuft
shashka	sabre
shelter-half	half a tent carried by one man
spatterdashes	gaiters (side-buttoned) reaching over the knee to protect stockings from mud
spats	short gaiter covering instep and reaching a little above the ankle
sporran	pouch, usually of fur, worn by Highlanders in front of kilt
stock	base of the barrel of a rifle
surcoat	loose robe worn over armour
surtout	greatcoat or frock coat
trews	trousers
tricorn hat	cocked hat with brim turned up on three sides
trimmings	ornamentation (lace, braid etc.) on uniforms
Ulanka	hussar tunic
vareuse	loose tunic (see *bluse*)
Waffenrock	campaign tunic
wideawake	broad-brimmed felt or straw hat

Select Bibliography

The following list represents a selection of the principal works about uniforms of land forces, arranged according to countries. The list concentrates particularly on the most recent literature. The bibliographies of the works mentioned contain a number of titles dealing with more specific subjects.

GENERAL READING

Cassin-Scott, Jack/Fabb, John   *Ceremonial Uniforms of the World*, London 1973

Cassin-Scott, Jack/Fabb, John   *Uniforms of the Napoleonic Wars*, London 1973

Colas, Rene   *Bibliographie générale des Costumes et la Mode* (Reprint), New York 1963

D'Armi, Rinaldo D.   *Les plus beaux Uniformes d'Europe*, Mailand/Paris 1966

D'Armi, Rinaldo D.   *World Uniforms in Colour*, Mailand/Paris 1969

Davenport, M.   *The Book of Costume*, New York 1962

Eckert, H. A./Monten, D.   *Sämtliche Truppen von Europa in charakteristischen Gruppen*, München/Würzburg 1838–1943

Falls, Cyril   *Great Military Battles*, London 1964

Fiebig, E.   *Husaren heraus! Reitergeist und Reitertat in Dolman und Attila*, Berlin 1933

Funcken, Liliane/Funcken, Fred   *Les Costumes et les Armes des Soldats de tous les Temps*, Brussels 1967

Funcken, Liliane/Funcken, Fred   *L'Uniforme et les Armes des Soldats de la Guerre 1914–18*, Tome 2, Brussels 1972

Funcken, Liliane/Funcken, Fred   *L'Uniforme et les Armes des Soldats de la Guerre 1939–45*, Brussels 1972

Funcken, Liliane/Funcken, Fred   *L'Uniforme et les Armes des Soldats de la Guerre en Dentelle*, Tome 2, Casterman 1975–6

Funcken, Liliane/Funcken, Fred   *L'Uniforme et les Armes des Soldats du premier Empire*, Tome 2, Brussels 1968–9

Haswell Miller, A. E./Dawney, N. P.   *Military Drawings and Paintings in the Collection of Her Majesty the Queen*, Vol. 2, London 1966 and 1970

Haythornthwaite, Philip   *Uniforms of Waterloo*, Poole 1976

Haythornthwaite, Philip   *World Uniforms and Battles 1815–1850*, Poole 1976

Kannik, Preben   *Alverdens Uniformer*, Kopenhagen 1967

Katalog der Lipperheideschen Kostümbibliothek, bearb. von E. Niessholdt u. G. Wagner-Neumann, 2 Bände, Berlin 1965

Knötel, Herbert   *Uniformkunde. Neue Folge*, Hamburg 1937

Knötel, Richard   *Mitteilungen zur Geschichte der militärischen Tracht*, Rathenow 1892–1921

Knötel, Richard/Knötel, Herbert   *Uniformkunde*, Rathenow 1890–1921, Neuauflage Hamburg 1932 und Krefeld ab 1965

Knötel, Richard/Knötel, Herbert/Sieg, Herbert   *Handbuch der Uniformkunde. Die militärische Tracht in ihrer Entwicklung bis zur Gegenwart*, Hamburg 1937, Nachdruck Hamburg 1956

Koenig, Otto   *Kultur und Verhaltensforschung. Einführung in die Kulturethologie*, München 1970

Lachouque, Henri   *Dix Siècles de Costume Militaire*, Paris 1965

Lefferts, Charles M.   *Uniforms of the American, British, French and German Armies in the War of the American Revolution 1775–1783*, Connecticut 1971

Lezius, Martin   *Das Ehrenkleid des Soldaten. Eine Kulturgeschichte der Uniform von ihren Anfängen bis zur Gegenwart*, Berlin 1936

Lippe, Ernst Graf zur   *Husaren–Buch*, Berlin 1863

Martin, Paul/Ullrich, Hans-Joachim   *Der Bunte Rock. Uniformen im Wandel der Zeiten*, Stuttgart 1963

Melegari, V.   *Great Regiments*, London 1969

Mollo, Andrew/McGregor, Malcolm   *Army Uniforms of World War 2*, London 1973

Mollo, Andrew/McGregor, Malcolm   *Naval, Marine and Air Force Uniforms of World War 2*, Poole, 1975

Mollo, John   *Military Fashion*, London 1972

Müller, Heinrich/Kunter, Fritz   *Europäische Helme aus der Sammlung des Museums für Deutsche Geschichte*, Berlin 1972

Nagyrévi v. Neppel, Georg   *Husaren*, Wiesbaden 1975

Nicholson, J. B. R.   *Military Uniforms*, London 1972

Pohler, Joh.   *Bibliotheca historico – militars*, Kassel 1887, Nachdruck New York 1961/62

Rosignoli, Guido   *Army Badges and Insignia of World War 2*, Vol. 2, Poole, 1972 and 1975

Rosignoli, Guido   *Army Badges and Insignia since 1945*, Poole 1973

Saxtorph, Niels M.   *Kriegstrachten in Farben*, Berlin 1971

Sussmann, Anton   *Die Armeen der Balkan-Staaten*, 3 Hefte, Leipzig 1914–1915

Toman, Karel   *Der Soldat im Wandel der Zeiten*, Hanau 1964

Wiener, Friedrich   *Felduniformen*, Heft 1, Koblenz 1974

Wiener, Friedrich   *Uniformen und Abzeichen*, 2 Hefete, Vienna 1973 and 1974

Wilbur, C. Keith   *Picture Book of the Continental Soldiers*, Harrisburg 1969

ARGENTINA

Evolution Historica de los Uniformes Argentinos, 1960

Uniformes de la patria, Buenos Aires 1972

AUSTRALIA

Festberg, Alfred N.   *Australian Army Insignia 1903–1966*, Bentleigh 1967

Festberg, Alfred N./Videan, Barry J.   *Uniforms of the Australian Colonies*, Melbourne 1972

AUSTRIA

Allmayer-Beck, Johann Christoph/Lessing, Erich   *Die k. (u.) k. Armee 1848–1914*, Vienna 1974

Dirrheimer, Günter   *Die k.k. Armee im Biedermeier*, Vienna 1975

Das Heer Maria Theresias, Faksimile-Ausgabe der Albertina – Handschrift "Dessins des Uniformes des Troupes I.I. et R.R. de l'année 1762", hrsg. und erläutert von Friedrich Kornauth, Vienna 1973

Mansfeld, J./Mansfeld, H.   *Militäruniformen der k. oesterreichischen Armee unter Erzherzog Karl*, Vienna 1805

Müller, F.   *Die kaiserl. königl. österreichische Armee seit Errichtung der stehenden Kriegsheere bis auf die neueste Zeit*, 2 Bände, Prag 1845

Patera, Herbert v.   *Unter Österreichs Fahnen*, Graz 1966

Schreiber, G.   *Des Kaisers Reiterei*, Vienna 1967

Seaton, Albert *Austro-Hungarian Army of the Napoleonic Wars*, Reading

Sussmann, Anton *Die österreich-ungarische Armee*, Leipzig 1910

Sussmann, Anton *Osterreichs Bundesheer*, Leipzig 1921

Teuber, Oskar/Ottenfeld, Rudolf v. *Die österreichische Armee von 1700–1861*, 2 Bände, Vienna 1895–1904

Wrede, A. v. *Unser Heer, 300 Jahre österreichisches Soldatentum in Krieg und Frieden*, Vienna 1909

Wrede, A. v. *Geschichte der k. u. k. Wehrmacht*, 4 Bände, Vienna 1898–1903

CHINA

Hill, J. C. *Die chinesische Armee in ihrer Neu-Uniformierung*, Leipzig 1912

DENMARK

Bruun, Chr. *Danske Uniformer*, Kopenhagen 1837

Hvidt, Anton *Danske Infanteris Uniformering og Oppakning genne de sidste 200 Ar*, Kopenhagen o. J.

FINLAND

Griepenberg, Ole: *Finsk Krigsmanna Beklädnad*. *Krigshistoriska* Samfundets Publikationer 2, Borga 1966

FRANCE

Brunon, R./Brunon, J. *L'Armée d'Afrique 1830–1962*, Salon-de-Provence 1976

Brunon, R./Brunon, J. *La Livre d'Or de la Légion Etrangère 1831–1976*, Salon-de-Provence 1976

Bucquoy, E. L. *Fanfares et Musiques des Troupes à Cheval*, Paris 1946

Bucquoy, E. L. *L'Uniforme à travers trois Siècles 1650–1920*, Paris 1945

Bucquoy, E. L. *Les Uniformes de L'Armée française (Terre-Mer-Air)*, Paris 1935

Cart, A. *Uniformes des Régiments Français de Louis XV à nos Jours*, Paris 1945

Dépréaux, A. *Costumes militaires de France au XVIIIe Siècle*, Paris 1945

Dépréaux, A. *L'Armée française 1939–1940*, Paris 1940

Dépréaux, A. *Les Uniforme des Troupes coloniales de 1666 à 1875*, Paris 1921

Detaill, Edourad/Richard, Jules *L'Armée française. Types et Uniformes*, Tome 2, Paris 1885–9

Fallow, F. *La Garde impériale (1804–1815)*, Paris 1901, Nachdruck Krefeld 1970

Galot, A./Robert, C. *Les Uniformes de l'Armée française de 1872 à 1914*, Tome 10, Paris 1967–1972

Grant, Charles *Foot Grenadiers of the Imperial Guard*, Reading 1971

Head, Michael G. *French Napoleonic Artillery*, London 1970

Head, Michael G. *French Napoleonic Lancer Regiments*, London 1971

Hourtouelle/Girbal *Soldats et Uniformes du Ier Empire*, Krefeld

Lienhardt/Humbert, R. *Les Uniformes de l'Armée française depuis 1690 à nos jours*, Tome 5, Leipzig 1897–1906

Malibran, H. *Guide à l'usage des artistes des costumiers contenant la description des uniformes de l'armée française de 1780 à 1848*, Paris 1904

Mangerand, J. *L'Armée française en 1845*, Paris 1945

Mangerand, J. *Les Coiffures de L'Armée française*, Paris 1904

Martin, Paul/Ullrich, Hans-Joachim *Soldaten im Bunten Rock. Die französische Armee 1789–1807*, Stuttgart 1969

Masson, F., *Cavaliers de Napoléon*, Paris 1895

Mouillard, L. *Les Régiments sous Louis XV*, Paris 1882

Notice descriptive des nouveaux Uniformes (30 mai 1919), hrsg. v. franz. Kriegsministerium, Paris 1920

Richard, Jules *La Garde impériale (1854–1870)*, Paris 1878

Rousselot, Lucïen *L'Armée française, ses Uniformes, son Armement, son Equipment*, Paris 1939–1976

Thorhurn, W. A. *French Army Regiments and Uniforms from the Revolution to 1870*, London 1969

Ullrich, Hans-Joachim *Soldaten im Bunten Rock. Die französische Armee 1789–1807*, Stuttgart 1969

Les uniformes de l'Armée française 1872–1918, Tome 8

GERMANY (see also PRUSSIA)

Davis, Brian L. *German Army Uniforms and Insignia 1933–1945*, London 1971

Denckler, Heinz *Abzeichen und Uniformen des Heeres*, Berlin 1943

Die Deutsche Reichswehr in ihrer neuesten Bekleidung, Bewaffnung und Ausrüstung, Leipzig 1934

Die Deutsche Soldatenkunde, hrsg. von B. Schwertfeger und E. O. Volkmann, 2 Bände, Leipzig 1936

Deutsche Heeresuniformen auf der Weltausstellung in Paris 1900 (1680–1863), Berlin 1900

Ehrlich, Curt *Uniformen und Soldaten. Ein Bildbericht vom Ehrenkleid unserer Wehrmacht*, Berlin 1942

Ellis, Chris *German Military Combat Dress 1939–1945*, London 1973

Erlam, Denys *Ranks and Uniform of the German Army–Navy–Airforce*, London 1939

Fosten, D. S. V. *Cuirassiers and Heavy Cavalry. Dress Uniforms of the German Imperial Cavalry 1900–1914*, New Malden 1972

Fosten, D. S. V./Marrion, R. J. *Waffen-SS. Its Uniforms, Insignia and Equipment 1938–1945*, London 1972

Hagger, D. H. *Hussars and Mounted Rifles. Uniforms of the German Cavalry 1900–1914*, New Malden 1974

Heer und Tradition. Die historische Uniformierung, Ausrüstung, Bewaffnung und Feldzeichen in der geschichtlichen Entwicklung von Heer, Kriegsmarine und Luftwaffe der Welt, hrsg. von Dr K. G. Klietmann, Berlin

Henckel, Karl *Atlas des Deutschen Reichsheeres und der Kaiserlichen Marine einschließlich der Kaiserlichen Schutztruppen in Afrika und des Ostasiatischen Expeditionscorps in ihrer Uniformierung und Einteilung dargestellt*, Dresden 1901

Hettler, Eberhard *Uniformen der Deutschen Wehrmacht. Heer, Kriegsmarine, Luftwaffe einschl. Nachtrag*, Berlin 1939 und 1940

Hiddemann, Fritz   *Uniformmaßschneidern für die Wehrmacht – eine Fachkunde auf der Grundlage der amtlichen Bekleidungs vorschriften*, Leipzig o. J.

Hoffschmidt, E./Tantum, W.   *German Army, Navy Uniforms and Insignia 1871–1918*, Reading

Hoyer, K./Brenneck, F.   *Die Uniformen des Reichsheeres und der deutschen Reichsmarine nebst amtlichen Uniformtafeln*, Berlin 1925

Jürgens, Hans   *Friedensuniformen des deutschen Heeres*, 2 Hefte, Hamburg 1954

Katalog der Lipperheideschen Kostümbibliothek bearb. von E. Niessholdt u. G. Wagner-Neumann, 2 Bände, Berlin 1965

Knötel, Herbert/Pietsch, Paul/Jantke, Egon/Collas, Baron   *Uniformenkunde. Das deutsche Heer. Friedensuniformen bei Ausbruch des Weltkrieges.* 3 Tafelbände, 1 Textband, von Paul Pietsch ergänzt, Hamburg 1935–61

Krickel, G./Lange, G.   *Das Deutsche Reichsheer in seiner neuesten Bekleidung und Ausrüstung*, Berlin 1888–90

Little John, David/Dodkins   *Orders, Decorations, Medals and Badges of the Third Reich*, Mountain View

Marrion, R. J./Fosten, D. S. V./Hagger, D. H.   *Lancers and Dragoons. Uniforms of the Imperial German Cavalry 1900–1914*, New Malden 1975

Mila, Adalbert   *Uniformierungsliste des Deutschen Reichsheeres und der Kaiserlich Deutschen Marine*, Berlin 1881

Mollo, Andrew   *Uniforms of the SS. Allgemeine SS 1923–1945*, London 1972

Mollo, Andrew   *Uniforms of the SS. SS-Verfügungstruppe 1933–1939*, London 1970

Mollo, Andrew   *Uniforms of the SS. SS-Totenkopfverbände 1933–1945*, London 1971

Mollo, Andrew   *Uniforms of the SS. Sicherheitsdienst und Sicherheitspolizei 1931–1945*, London 1971

Mollo, Andrew   *Uniforms of the SS. Waffen-SS, Clothing and Equipment 1939–1945*, London 1972

Mollo, Andrew/Taylor, Hugh Page   *Uniforms of the SS. Germanische SS 1940–1945*, London 1970

Osten-Sacken/v. Rhein   *Deutschlands Armee in feldgrauer Kriegs- und Friedens-uniform*, Berlin 1916

Schulz, Wolfharti   *Bekleidungswesen*, Hamburg 1974

Transfeldt, Walter/Brand, Karl Hermann Frhr. v./Quenstedt, Otto   *Wort und Brauch im deutschen Heer. Allerlei Militärisches, was mancher nicht weiß*, Hamburg 1976

Wacker, Peter   *Deutsche Uniformen aus zwei Jahrhunderten*, Bad Godesberg, 1967

Windrow, Martin D.   *The Panzer Divisions*, Reading

Windrow, Martin D.   *Waffen-SS*, Reading

BAVARIA

Cantler, Johann Baptist/Wrede   *Der Bayerischen Armee sämtliche Uniformen von 1800–1873*, Schwarzbach o.J.

Hoffmann, A.   *Das Heer des blauen Königs. Die Bayerische Armee unter dem Kurfürst Max II. Emanuel von 1682–1728*, Schwarzbach o.J.

Müller, Karl/Braun, Louis   *Die Organisation, Bekleidung, Ausrüstung und Bewaffnung der Königlich Bayerischen Armee von 1806 bis 1906*, Schwarzbach o.J.

BRUNSWICK

Pivka, Otto von   *The Black Brunswickers*, Reading

HANOVER

Pivka, Otto von   *The King's German Legion*, Reading 1974

HESSE

Metz, Ernst   *Hessische Uniformen der Biedermeierzeit, 1825–1845*, Kassel 1961

HESSE-DARMSTADT

Kredel, Fr.   *Die Uniformen der Hessen-Darmstädtischen Infanterie*, Darmstadt 1940

PRUSSIA

Bleckwenn, Hans   *Das Altpreußische Heer, Erscheinungsbild und Wesen*, Osnabrück 1970

Bleckwenn, Hans   *Die Okonomie – Reglements des altpreußischen Heeres 1713–1806*, Osnabrück 1973

Bleckwenn, Hans   *Urkunden und Kommentare zur Entwicklung der altpreußischen Uniform als Erscheinungsbild und gesellschaftliche Manifestation*, Osnabrück 1970

Bleckwenn, Hans/Melzner, F.-G.   *Die Dessauer Spezifikation von 1729*, Osnabrück 1971

Bleckwenn, Hans/Melzner, F.-G.   *Die Uniformen der Infanterie 1753–1786*, Osnabrück 1973

Deutsche Heeresuniformen auf der Weltausstellung in Paris 1900 (1680–1863), Berlin 1900

Duffy, Christopher/Elzholz, L./Rechlin, C./Schulz, J.   *The Army of Frederick the Great*, London 1974. *Das Preußische Heer*, Berlin 1830–1836

Hammer, F. W.   *Das Königlich Preußische Heer in seiner gegenwärtigen Uniformierung*, Berlin 1862–1865

Horvarth, Karl Christian   *Friedrich II. König von Preußen, Armee-Montierungen*, Potsdam 1789

Horvarth, Karl Christian   *Preußische Armee-Uniformen unter der Regierung Friedrich Wilhelms II*, Potsdam 1789

Jany, Curt   *Geschichte der Preußischen Armee vom 15. Jahrhundert bis 1914*, 4 Bände, Nachdruck, Osnabrück 1967

Kling, C(onstantin)   *Geschichte der Bekleidung, Bewaffnung und Ausrüstung des Kgl. Preußischen Heeres*, 3 Teile, Weimar 1902, 1906 und 1912. Teil Nachdruck Osnabrück 1971

Krause, Gisela   *Altpreußische Uniformanfertigung als Vorstufe der Bekleidungsindustrie*, Hamburg 1965

Krippenstapel, Fr./Knötel, Richard   *Die preußischen Husaren von den ältesten Zeiten bis zur Gegenwart*, Berlin 1883, Nachdruck Krefeld o. J.

Lange, E.   *Heerschau Friedrichs des Großen*, Leipzig 1856

Lange, E.   *Die Soldaten Friedrichs des Großen*, Leipzig 1853

Lehmann, G.   *Forschungen und Urkunden zur Geschichte der Uniformierung der Preußischen Armee 1713–1807*, I. Teil, Berlin 1900

Melzner, F.-G.   *Die Dessauer Spezifikation von 1737*, Osnabrück

Menzel, Adolph v.   *Die Armee Friedrichs des Großen in ihrer*

Uniformierung, gezeichnet und erläutert, 10 Lieferungen, Berlin
Mila, Adalbert *Geschichte der Bekleidung und Ausrüstung der Königlich Preußischen Armee in den Jahren 1808–1878*, Berlin 1878, Nachdruck Krefeld o.J.
Ortenburg, Georg *Preußische Husarenbilder um 1791*, Kopenhagen 1976
Pelet-Narbonne, G. *Geschichte der brandenburgisch-preußischen. Reiterei*, Berlin 1905
Pietsch, Paul *Die Formations und Uniformierungsgeschichte des preußischen Heeres 1808–1914*, 2 Bände Hamburg 1963 und 1966
Rabe, E. *Uniformen des Preußischen Heeres in ihren Hauptveränderungen bis auf die Gegenwart*, Berlin 1846
Schindler, C. F. *Militar-Album des Kgl. Preuß. Heeres*, Berlin 1862
S(chmalen), I. C. H. v. *Akkurate Vorstellung der sämtlichen Königlich Preußischen Armee*, Nürnberg 1759, 1762, 1770, 1777, 1779, 1783 und 1787
Schwarze, Wolfgang *Die Uniformen der Preußischen Garden von ihrer Entstehung 1704 bis 1836*, Wuppertal 1975
Seaton, Albert *Frederick the Great's Army*, Reading
Thieme, Johann Georg *Genaue Zeichnung und Beschreibung Säntlicher Uniformen der Königlich Preußischen Armee 1792*
(Thümen, v.) *Die Uniformen der Preußischen Garden von ihrem Enstehen bis auf die neueste Zeit, nebst einer kurzen Darstellung ihrer verschiedenen Formationen 1704–1836*, Berlin 1827–1840
Ullrich, Hans-Joachim *Soldaten im Bunten Rock. Die preußische Armee unter Friedrich Wilhelm II. und Friedrich Wilhelm III, 1786–1807*, Stuttgart 1968
Ullrich, Hans-Joachim *Soldaten im Bunten Rock. Die preußische Armee 1808–1839*, Stuttgart 1970
Ullrich, Hans-Joachim *Soldaten im Bunten Rock. Die preußische Armee 1840–1871*, Stuttgart 1972
Uniforms of the Seven Years War. No. 1 Prussia, Thornaby-on-Tees 1974
Young. Peter *Blücher's Army*, Reading 1973
SAXONY
Dietrich. Walther *Die Uniformen der Kurfürstlich und Königl. Sächsischen Armee 1672–1914*, Leipzig 1921
Hauthal, F. *Geschichte der Sächsischen Armee in Wort und Bild*, Leipzig 1859
GREAT BRITAIN
Barnes, R. Money *A History of the Regiments and Uniforms of the British Army*, London o. J.
Barnes, R. Money *Military Uniforms of Britain and the Empire, 1742 to the Present Time*, London 1960
Barnes, R. Money *The Uniforms and History of the Scottish Regiments of Britain, Canada, Australia, New Zealand and South Africa, 1625 to the Present Day*, London 1960
Blandford, W. *British Uniforms*, London 1914
Blaxland, Gregory *The Buffs*, Reading
Bloomer, W. H./Bloomer, K. D. *Scottish Regimental Badges 1793–1971*, London

Bowling, H. *British Hussar Regiments*, London 1972
Bryant, A. *The Age of Elegance 1812–1822*, London 1952
Campbell, D. A. *Dress of the Royal Artillery*, London 1971
Carman, W. Y. *British Military Uniforms from Contemporary Pictures, Henry VII to the Present Day*, London 1957
Carman, W. Y. *Glengarry Badges of the British Line Regiments to 1881*, London
Carman, W. Y. *Head Dresses of the British Army, Cavalry*, Sutton 1968
Carman, W. Y. *Head Dresses of the British Army, Yeomanry*, Sutton 1970
Carman, W. Y. *Royal Artillery*, Reading
Carman, W. Y. *Sabretaches of the British Army*, London 1969
Dawson, Malcolm *Uniforms of the Royal Armoured Corps*, London 1974
Embleton, Gerald *Wolfe's Army*, Reading
Grant, Charles *The Black Watch*, Reading
Grant, Charles *The Coldstream Guards*, Reading
Grant, Charles *Royal Scots Greys*, Reading
Holding, T. H. *Uniforms of the British Army, Navy and Court*, London 1894, Reprint 1969
Kipling, Arthur L./King, Hugh L. *Head-Dress Badges of the British Army*, London 1974
Laver, James *British Military Uniforms*, London 1948
Lawson, Cecil C. P. *A History of the Uniforms of the British Army*, Vol. 5, London 1940–1967
May, W. E./Carman, W. Y./Tanner, J. *Badges and Insignia of the British Armed Services*, London 1974
McElwee, William *Argyll and Sutherland Highlanders*, Reading
Nevill, Ralph *British Military Prints*, London 1909
Pivka, Otto von *The King's German Legion*, Reading 1974
Selby, John *The Iron Brigade*, Reading
Selby, John *The Stonewall Brigade*, Reading
Shepperd, Alan *The Connaught Rangers*, Reading
Shepperd, Alan *The King's Regiment*, Reading
Simkins, Peter *Regiments of Scottish Division*, Basingstoke
Stadden, Charles *Coldstream Guards. Dress and Appointments 1658–1972*, London 1973
Stadden, Charles *The Life Guards*, London 1973
Strachow, H. *British Military Uniforms 1768–96*, London 1975
Telfer Dunbar, John *History of Highland Dress*, Edinburgh 1962
Thorburn, W. A. *Uniforms of the Scottish Infantry*, Edinburgh 1970
Wilkinson, F. *Badges of the British Army 1820–1960*
Wilkinson, F. *Cavalry and Yeomanry Badges of the British Army 1914*, London 1973
Wilkinson-Latham. Robert/Wilkinson-Latham. Christopher *Cavalry Uniforms*, London 1969
Wilkinson-Latham, Robert/Wilkinson-Latham,

Christopher *Infantry Uniforms 1742–1939*, Vol. 2, London 1969 and 1970
Wilson, Frank *Regiments at a Glance*, London 1956
HUNGARY (see under AUSTRIA)
Szendrei, J. *Magyar viseletek történeti fejlödése*, Budapest 1905
INDIA
Carman, W. Y. *Indian Army Uniforms under the British from the 18th Century to 1947*, Vol. 2, London 1961 and 1969
Jackson, D. *India's Army*, London 1940
ITALY
Gasparinetti, Alessandro *L'Uniforme Italiana nella Storia e nell'Arte*, Rome 1961
Guidice, Elio/Guidice, Vittorio *Uniformi Militari Italiane dal 1861 ai Giorni Nostri*, Vol. 2, Mailand 1964
Matt, Leonard von *Die päpstliche Schweizergarde*, Zürich 1948
Repond *Le Costume de la Garde pontificale et la Renaissance italienne*, Rome 1917
JAPAN
Nakata, Tadao *Imperial Japanese Army and Navy Uniform and Equipment*, Tokyo 1973
Warner, Philip *The Japanese Army of World War II*, Reading
JORDAN
Young, Peter *The Arab Legion*, Reading
MEXICO
Hefter, Nieto/Brown *The Mexikan Soldier 1837–1847, Organisation, Dress and Equipment*, Mexico 1958
NETHERLANDS
Cats, B. C./Coenders, C. P. *Netherlands Army Regimental Badges*
Fortes Wels, P. *De Nederlandse Cavalerie*, Bussum 1963
Hohmann, J. *Die Niederländische Armee nebst Kolonialtruppen*, Leipzig 1906
Yperen, R. van *De Nederlandse Militaire Musiek, Bussum 1966*
NORWAY
Den Norske Haer, Leipzig 1932
POLAND
Linder, Karel/Wiewiora, H./Woznicki, T. *Zolniers Polski Ubiar Uzbrojenie I Oporzadzenie od 1939 de 1964*, 4 Bände, Warsaw 1965
RUMANIA
Uniformele Armati Romane 1830–1930. Bukarest 1930
SPAIN
Bueno, J. M. *Uniformes Militares en color de la Guerra Civil Espānola*, Madrid
Ferrer, F./Heftes, J. *Bibliografia iconografico del Traje Militar de Espāna*, Mexico 1963
SWEDEN
Dalbeck, A. *Svenska Uniformer och Fälttegn, Band 1: Garde och Rytteri 1885–1965*, Stockholm o. J.

SWITZERLAND
Petitmermet, R./Rousselot, G. *Schweizer Uniformen 1700–1850*, Bern 1976
Schneider, Hugo *Vom Harnisch zum Waffenrock 1650–1915*, Zürich 1968
Sommerfeld, F. *Die Schweizer Armee, ihre Bewaffnung, Uniformen und Abzeichen*, Leipzig 1915
USA
Eltring, John R. *Military Uniforms in America. The Era of the American Revolution 1755–1795*, San Rafael, Cal. 1974
Grosvenor, Gilbert *Insignia and Decorations of the U.S. Armed Forces*, Washington 1945
Gurney, Gene *A Pictorial History of the United States Army*, New York 1966
Kredel, Fritz/Todd, Frederick *Soldiers of the American Army*, Chicago 1950
Lord, F./Wise, A. *Uniforms of the Civil War*, New York 1970
Mollo, John/MacGregor, Malcolm *Uniforms of the American Revolution*, Poole 1975
Ogden, H. *Uniforms of the United States Army*, Vol. 2, Göttingen 1907
Ogden, H./Nelson, Henry Loomis *Uniforms of the United States Army, First Series (1779–1888)*, New York 1960
Ogden, H./Pakula, Marvin H. *Uniforms of the United States Army, Second Series (1898–1907)*, New York 1960
Selby, John *The United States Marine Corps*, Reading
Selby, John *U.S. Cavalry*, Reading
Windrow, Martin/Embleton, George *Military Dress of North America 1665–1970*
Young, Peter *George Washington's Army*, Reading
USSR
Curtiss, J. S. *The Russian Army under Nicholas I, 1825–1855*, Durham, N.C. 1965
Gayda, M./Krijitsky, A. *L'Armée Russe sous le Tsar Alexandre Ier*, Paris 1955
Harintonov, O. V. *Uniforms and Marks of Distinction (Insignia) of the Soviet Army 1918–1958*, Leningrad 1958
Red Army Uniforms and Insignia 1944, London 1974
Rottmann, Hans *Die russische Armee in ihren gegenwärtigen Uniformen*, Leipzig 1912
Seaton, Albert *The Cossacks*, Reading 1972
Seaton, Albert *The Russian Army of the Crimea*, Reading
Seaton, Albert *The Soviet Army*, Reading
Seaton, Albert/Youens, Michael *The Russian Army of the Napoleonic Wars*, Reading 1973
Soviet Army Uniforms and Insignia 1945–1975, London 1975
Stein, F. v. *Geschichte des Russischen Heeres*, 3 Bände, Nachdruck Krefeld 1975
Viskovatov, A. V. *Historische Beschreibung der Uniformen und Bewaffnung der russischen Armee*, 50 Bände, St Petersburg 1844–56
Zweguintzow, W. *L'Armée Russe*, 2 Bände, Paris 1967 und 1969

Index

Acknowledgments

The editor would particularly like to thank Robert Spiering of *Der Spiegel* and John Mollo for their help in preparing this book.

Photographs were supplied or reproduced by kind permission of the following:

By gracious permission of Her Majesty the Queen: *50–1, 142*
The Ann S. K. Brown Military Collection: 181
Bildarchiv Preussischer Kulturbesitz, Berlin: 101, 132
Hans Bleckwenn Archives: 9, 10, 11, 33, 37, 40, 43
Bulloz: 75, 104–5
Canadian Forces Photographs: 228–9
Colonial Williamsburg Foundation: 69
Domaine de Grosbois: *98–9*
Fotomas Index: 177
The Goodwood Collection: 52
Historical Picture Service: 14–15, *182–3*, 184–5, 188, *198, 199*
Imperial War Museum: 209, 211, 212, 215, 219, 220
Library of Congress: 56–7, 66–7
Mansell Collection: 168–9, 172
Paul Martin Collection: 73, 74, 77, 80, 84, 88, 88–9, *94, 95*
Militärverlag der DDR: 241

Mollo Collection: 159
Musée de l'Armée, Paris: endpapers
National Army Museum: *143*, 144, 147, 148, 149, 151, 152–3, 154
The Trustees, The National Gallery, London: 61
Pennsylvania Academy: 47
J. Player & Sons: 205
Clichés Musées Nationaux Paris: *26–7, 62–3*, 108, 109, *134–5, 173, 178*
Roger-Viollet: 196
G. Rosignoli Collection: 208, 236
Royal Yugoslav Combatants' Association: 229
Soldier Magazine: 243
Somerset County Museum: 141
Staatsgalerie, Stuttgart: *82–3*
US Army Photographs: 222–3
Versailles: *24–5*
Weidenfeld and Nicolson archives: 160–1
Zeughauses, Berlin: 2–3

Numbers in italics indicate colour photographs.